"In a rushed world, people need spiritual guidance that is concise and realistic. *Reality Check* is both."

John Ortberg, Teaching Pastor
Willow Creek Community Church

"The wit and wisdom in this book provide a welcome tonic of sanity mixed with timeless scriptural truth."

Timothy C. Morgan, Deputy Managing Editor,
Christianity Today Magazine

"Kudos to Verla Gillmor for her pithy, power-packed take on living anthentically for God."

Jane Johnson Struck,
Managing Editor, *Today's Christian Woman*

"With her wealth of experience as a successful businesswoman, Verla speaks with a 'been-there-done-that' voice and . . . emphasizes the practical application of God's Word to our hurried, crowded lives."

Mary Welchel, author, radio host and speaker
Founder, *The Christian Working Woman*

"*Reality Check,* with its buoyant wit and zest for heavenly wisdom, absolutely merits your reading and reevaluation. Don't miss it!"

Dr. Bruce McNicol
President, Leadership Catalyst Inc.,
Co-author, *The Ascent of a Leader*

"*Reality Check* gives God room to turn the spotlight from our circumstances to the state of the heart. Enjoy!"

Esther Burroughs, Aspiring Women speaker
Author of *A Garden Path to Mentoring, Splash the Living Water* and *Empowered*

"Verla Gillmor brings her experience in the media world, corporate world and real-life world to address my own heart issues. *Reality Check* is deeply spiritual and nakedly real. I highly recommend it."

Dr. Stacy T. Rinehart, CEO, MentorLink.org
Author of *Upside Down: The Paradox of Servant Leadership*

"*Reality Check* is a powerful reminder that true devotion to God can be cultivated in the trenches of twenty-first century living."

Nichole Johnson, Women of Faith speaker
Author of *Fresh-Brewed Life*

"Is authentic faith possible today in our fast, tough, modern world? What would Jesus do? If you want to take a hard look at these questions, read on. This book has some surprising answers."

Karen Brugler, Project Director, Leadership Curriculum
The Good Samaritan Society

"*Reality Check* . . . goes straight to the heart of the matter with writing and illustrations that bring the principles front and center."

Don Stephens
President & CEO, Mercy Ships International

"This book calls us away from mediocrity in our daily devotions to a deeper relationship with God . . . a thought-provoking read."

Joanne Hawes, President and Founding Director
Life Purpose Ministries

REALITY CHECK

REALITY CHECK

A Survival Manual for
Christians in the Workplace

Verla Gillmor

HORIZON BOOKS
CAMP HILL, PENNSYLVANIA

HORIZON BOOKS

3825 Hartzdale Drive, Camp Hill, PA 17011
www.cpi-horizon.com
www.christianpublications.com

Reality Check: A Survival Manual for Christians in the Workplace
ISBN: 0-88965-195-7
LOC Control Number: 00-135128
© 2001 by Horizon Books
All rights reserved
Printed in the United States of America

01 02 03 04 05   5 4 3 2 1

For my daughter, Lisa

who is a constant reminder that
God gives us more than we deserve

CONTENTS

PART ONE:
Taming Our Inner World

Ambition

Anger

Arrogance

Disappointment

Drift

Envy

Failure

Fear

Identity

PART TWO:
Taming Our Outer World

PART THREE:
Spiritual Flashpoints

Acknowledgments

Circus performers say that when a trapeze artist jumps off his pedestal and lets go of the trapeze, he must stretch out his arms with absolute trust, believing the catcher will catch him. He must never try to grab the catcher. The partnership works well only when both parties know their roles.

Writing this book, I've flung my thoughts with great conviction upon each page, trusting God would "catch" the words and take them where they need to go. Without the Catcher, I knew the words would sink like a rock. This book in your hands is proof He's been faithful. My heart is full of thanks.

I'm also deeply indebted to Editorial Director George McPeek for championing this book early on and for striking just the right balance of encouragement and truth-telling whenever I faltered. An equal measure of gratitude goes to Marilynne Foster, whose skilled editing accomplished what every writer hopes for—an improved manuscript without the loss of the writer's "voice."

Although writing, in the end, is a solitary activity, no one writes alone. My mother, Eleanor Thurman, and siblings, Eric Thurman, Starr Thurman and Sonya Harkins, exceeded the bounds of family support—especially Eric, whose computer rescues have earned him a special spot in the Brother Hall of Fame.

I'm also grateful for the women who have been my day-in-day-out support on this project: Judy Keene (especially you, my friend), Kathie Tack, Karen Brugler, Esther Hall and Lois Albrecht. Their love, wise counsel and excessive grace are a tribute to the word "community."

Thanks, too, to the women in my entrepreneurs' small group and the leaders with whom I serve in the LifeWork career seminars at Willow Creek Community Church. Your prayers and "atta girls" are deeply appreciated.

Then, there are my friends-for-life, Beth Krusich, Jan Adams and Carol Montgomery, with whom I enjoy a lifelong bond of love and support. You have stood with me in all the seasons of my life—including this one—and I don't know what I'd do without you.

Finally, to my daughter, Lisa Martinson, whose wisdom runs deep and whose love and loyalty defies rational explanation. Your support means the world. I'm so glad to be your mom.

Introduction

I've greatly benefited from the words of Christian contemplatives written down through the ages. Sometimes, though, I find myself talking back to them. "Hey, walk a mile in my moccasins and *then* see how you feel about patience!" Or "It's easy for you to say you love everybody. Try working for *my* boss and see how lovable you feel!" The problem with life in the real world is that it's nasty out there.

My favorite Bible characters are the ones who got banged up physically, mentally, emotionally and spiritually as they tried to live out their faith. That's what life looks like for most of us. Jacob is a good example. His résumé is hardly pristine. He didn't always get it right. He wrestled with God and walked the rest of his life with a limp. But, in the end, he learned firsthand that God was worth following, whatever the cost. He didn't have a shrink-wrapped faith.

Let's face it. A vibrant relationship with God is messy. When Michelangelo created his magnificent *David* sculpture, he reportedly was asked, "How did you know what David should look like?" He replied, "I just cut away everything that wasn't David."

Living a transparent, authentic life of faith means allowing the Holy Spirit to cut away everything that isn't us—the "us" God intended. Spiritual growth has to get personal. God's truth has to grab us by the lapels and get in our face.

God is not Mr. Rogers. He's not satisfied to "chat up" the Christian life like a talk show guest sandwiched between "Tips for Cleaning Your Carpet" and "How to Buy Life Insurance." He is out to disturb our comfort zones, challenge our perceptions and excise the world's nastiness from our souls, loving us passionately every step of the way.

If you yearn to find God active at the intersection of faith and real life, there's good news. That's where He lives. I hope this book will be encouragement for the journey.

Verla Gillmor

PART ONE:

Taming Our Inner World

The Terror of Being Average

We live in a culture obsessed with accomplishment—from the extraordinary to the just plain bizarre. In Cieza, Spain, a man spit an olive pit more than sixty-nine feet. A fellow competitor said admiringly, "You don't see someone with lungs like that every day."

At the National Hollerin' Contest in Spiveys Corner, North Carolina, Gregory Jackson took top honors one year for his four-minute hollering rendition of "Amazing Grace." Kinda makes you feel warm all over, doesn't it?

On the other hand, Stacy Allison's conquest of Mt. Everest ranks as a bona fide heroic accomplishment. Reports of her terrifying descent while battling snow blindness and lack of oxygen are nothing short of riveting. "On a steep slope just below the summit," TIME magazine reported, "she leaned over to see a foothold through the blazing retinal glare. The empty oxygen tank overbalanced her. She somersaulted downward, swung her ice ax, stuck it into the snow face and performed a perfect self-arrest. 'Being in peril,' she says, 'sharpens your sense of life.' "

Yes, Stacy, if I were falling off Mt. Everest, I would be *very* alert.

In each of these stories someone wanted to set himself apart from the pack. Extraordinary achievement telegraphs that we're not here on the planet simply to take up space.

I'm embarrassed to admit that ambition has more than once sucked me into its vortex. One incident is forever seared in my memory because of the danger in which I put myself and my family. It happened during my early years as a reporter working for a network radio affiliate in Chicago.

Chicago is a wonderful city to ply your trade if you're a journalist. Chicagoans take their news very seriously. However, there's heavy competition among media outlets to "break" a story or to gain an "exclusive."

The incident took place around the time Puerto Rican FALN (Armed Forces of National Liberation) terrorists had bombed several local buildings as a political protest in their fight to win independence for Puerto Rico. The damage was nothing of the magnitude of the Oklahoma City bombing several years later. Nevertheless, they were driving federal law enforcement officials crazy because they kept eluding capture.

One day, two of the group's minor players were arrested when they were stopped for a routine traffic violation. They were taken to the Criminal Court Building and held for arraignment. One of my sources called to tip me off that they were in custody and offered to get me into their cell for an interview.

The man everybody *really* wanted to interview was Oscar Lopez Rivera, the leader of the small but active band of zealots. So, after my brief and not-that-groundbreaking interview with the two lower-echelon terrorists, I handed them my business card, wrote my home phone number on the back and told them I would be willing to meet with Rivera anytime for an interview—if he were interested.

When I got back to the newsroom, I rushed in to tell the news director about the interview and my offer to meet with Rivera.

"You what?" he said incredulously. "You gave your home phone number to a terrorist? Are you a complete idiot? I should fire you on the spot!"

Fortunately, I'm sure Oscar Lopez Rivera wasn't the least bit interested in me. If he wanted a blockbuster interview, he'd have gone to Dan Rather. What was I thinking? The operative words are "blind ambition."

When is ambition a good thing, and when is it a problem? Eugene Peterson says it's a problem when, somewhere along the way, aspiration and impatience with mediocrity—which are good—turn into something unruly—ambition without qualification.

In his book, *A Long Obedience in the Same Direction*, Peterson says,

> Ambition is aspiration gone crazy. Aspiration is the channeled, creative energy that moves us to growth in Christ, shaping goals in the Spirit. Ambition takes these same energies for growth and development and uses them to make something tawdry and cheap, sweatily knocking together a Babel when we could be vacationing in Eden.[1]

It's ironic that, for all our posturing for position, God has never been interested in focusing on "the best and the brightest" in the human gene pool to get His work done on earth. The ground is level at the foot of the cross. Diplomas and titles and accomplishments get checked at the door.

I don't get it. Jesus could have gotten His kingdom here on earth off to a much better start if He had picked twelve disciples who weren't such losers. I read the gospels and think, *We need heroes! We want role models! Where are their credentials? Would you look at those pathetic résumés!*

Then I stumble onto Acts 4 where Peter and John, ignited by the Holy Spirit, appear before the Sanhedrin, Israel's Supreme Court. Luke, the author of Acts, describes a crowd that is totally captivated—for reasons that have nothing to do with their credentials or dazzling presentation.

The Bible says, "When they saw the courage of Peter and John and realized that they were unschooled, ordinary men, they were astonished and they took note that these men had been with Jesus" (Acts 4:13).

Peter and John were not educated. They were not part of the religious cognoscenti. But they had been with Jesus. That was their defining credential. People sat up and took notice. Their lives mattered.

These days, I hold my gifts and abilities loosely. They're a nice perk of being *me*, but they aren't the main point. The main point is how much have I been with Jesus.

Reality

☐ Are you ambitious?

☐ Would you describe your ambition as Spirit-controlled or out of control?

☐ Name three goals that currently motivate you to excel.

☐ Are they compatible with God's values and priorities for your life?

☐ How will others remember you when you are gone?

☐ Have you "been with Jesus" enough for it to show?

Warning: Contents Explode under Pressure

nger scares me. It roars in, bigger than I expect, and doesn't leave quietly. In an instant, it affects everything in its wake.

During my years in Chicago broadcasting, I was given the chance to work for NBC's top-rated radio station. The job catapulted me into broadcasting's big leagues, and I was determined to work hard and wow everybody with my excellent reporting skills.

One of my first assignments was a "breaking" story of a pleasure boat that sank in a sudden storm on Lake Michigan. Several passengers onboard had drowned. The Coast Guard dramatically rescued the rest. I raced to the scene where a Coast Guard cutter was bringing survivors ashore, hoping to grab interviews and hurry back to the station to get the story on the air as quickly as possible.

My editor, a belligerent fellow with more than twenty years at NBC, had a reputation for making miserable the lives of on-air staffers—especially the women. Humiliation and intimidation were his weapons of choice. He managed to keep his job, despite his hostility, because he was an excellent editor who would give his life for the job. Bosses like that.

As I scrambled to finish my report for the fast-approaching newscast, he seized on the fact that, in my rush to file the story, I failed to get the Coast Guard spokesman's first name. It was a careless error on my part but not one that merited what happened next.

The editor stood in the middle of the newsroom in the front of about a dozen people and began shouting personal insults at me in the ugliest display of meanness I have ever experienced. Finally, he turned and walked out. I stood frozen in place like a deer caught in the headlights.

Anger is one of those emotions we call bad if it's directed *at* us and justified if it comes *from* us. In truth, anger, as an emotion, isn't good *or* bad. It's just one of the wide range of human emotions. It's what we do with anger that gets us in trouble.

Jesus used anger selectively and with great impact to lash out at hypocrisy and injustice and express disappointment at sin. We, on the other hand, indiscriminately fling it out like a hand grenade at the person who cuts in front of us to grab the last parking space.

That's probably why the Bible considers self-control a highly prized character trait. We need self-control to keep anger in its proper place. Proverbs 29:11 says, "A fool gives full vent to his anger, but a wise man keeps himself under control."

Self-control isn't handed to us as an instant "up-grade" when we join the family of faith. It's produced in us by the Holy Spirit as we invest time in our spiritual development.

I'm not an angry, hot-tempered person. I hate conflict. Nevertheless, my blood can boil as fast as the next person's over some perceived "wrong." Patient understanding is not my most natural posture.

When I feel anxiety rising, my first line of defense is to send up my favorite prayer—"Help!" I force myself to take several long deep breaths, silently count to ten and remind myself that the way to end conflict is seldom to return fire. Later, when I'm removed from the situation I think, *What will help me handle this person or this situation differently if it comes up again? What is my anger saying about what I need or want?*

Sometimes, to be honest, I don't get past "Help!"

First Samuel 25 illustrates the right way and the wrong way of handling an explosive situation. A simple request rapidly escalated into a potential disaster because of a surly, big-mouthed farmer named Nabal and David's hotheaded response to him. Their combined anger could have spelled disaster if God had not sent help.

David and 600 soldiers loyal to him were on the run from King Saul because Saul feared David as a rival for his throne. While on the run, David had the formidable task of finding food and water every day for his troops. It wasn't easy since they weren't ever in one place very long. One way David met the need was to protect the land and flocks of wealthy farmers like Nabal from raiders. In return, David would ask for compensation or provisions from the farmers.

Nabal had no interest in helping David. "Who is this David? . . . Why should I take my bread and water, and the meat I have slaughtered for my shearers, and give it to men coming from who knows where?" (25:10-11).

When Nabal's response got back to David, he told 400 of his men to grab their swords because they were going to show Nabal a thing or two. (David will never be accused of doing anything halfheartedly.)

Fortunately, Nabal's beautiful and intelligent wife, Abigail, sprang into action. She knew her husband was a mean man who would not back down, and she knew David deserved compensation. So she sent servants with provisions to meet David, and she rode her donkey out to greet him personally before he reached Nabal.

"Ignore Nabal," she said. "He's a fool" (25:25, author's paraphrase). "Let no wrongdoing be found in you as long as you live" (25:28). She assured David that if he acted wisely now, when he became king he would "not have on his conscience the staggering burden of needless bloodshed" (25:31).

To his credit, David recognized that Abigail was sent by God to stop him from doing something stupid. "May you be blessed for your good judgment," he told her, "and for keeping me from bloodshed this day" (25:33).

In a way, God's still in the business of keeping us from doing something stupid. The Holy Spirit can place a "check" in our spirits when we're headed for trouble with swords drawn. But we have to be willing to listen.

Reality

☐ How do you deal with your anger and with other people's anger directed at you?

☐ Are there certain situations that trigger anger in you or others—such as an overloaded schedule with no margin or a careless personal habit that you know upsets those around you?

☐ Are you willing to present these circumstances to God and ask for help?

Upsizing Me

Arrogance is hot. In fact, advertising—which taps into our deepest felt needs and desires—thrives on arrogance. "Make your own road," one car ad exults. Another luxury car ad says, "Go places. Come back. Gloat." Women are urged to buy a certain hair product because, "You're worth it." Burgers are now fixed "your way."

If you're worth it, by implication somebody else is not worth it. That means the other guy has got to move over or, better yet, take his place beneath you since *you* know what's best.

I submitted an essay once to a prestigious literary magazine in New York City. I felt very brave, knowing the chances of it receiving acceptance were slim or none. After several weeks without a response, I called to follow up. A haughty, patronizing voice delivered the voice mail message: "If you *must* leave a message, (deep sigh) do so after the tone" (click). No "Have a nice day." No "Your call is important to us." (Even though that's the message I hate the most, it was starting to sound pretty good at that point.)

Undeterred, I placed a follow-up call to the editor who screens essays. His voice mail message said, "Don't bother leaving a message. We don't listen to them" (click).

I understand that voice mail has become the new firewall between busy people and the teeming masses but . . . puhleeeze . . . what's with the attitude?

This is not the part of the book where I trot out a self-righteous diatribe about the arrogance of the rich and famous and pontificate how pride goes before a fall, blah, blah, blah. The rich, the famous and the powerful may have a platform and the means to dish out arrogance in bigger doses and get away with it, but they certainly don't own the franchise.

Arrogance debuted in the Garden of Eden when Eve decided she knew better than God what was best. Down through history, "I know what's best" has spawned off-spring like, "When I want your advice, I'll ask for it," "I'm better than you," "I'm right, and you're wrong" and the ever-popular ". . . because I said so."

Every kid who's been beat up at least once by a bully on the playground learns you can't just say those things flat out or you end up with a bloody nose. But we find ways. When our response includes a muddy mixture of both good and bad motives, it makes the arrogance harder to spot.

My own struggle in this area is with my writing. I want to be profound. It's honestly not because my ego demands that I be seen as some sort of brilliant person. My friends and my own insecurities keep my feet firmly planted on the ground in that regard. It's that I can't bear to write something "trivial."

Life's too short. There's too much at stake. Since people read so few books, I want their time to be well spent reading this one. I can't bear the thought of writing words that won't move people to tear up their preconceived notions and look at life differently. I want the writing to matter because life is hard, and we need all the help we can get.

So what's wrong with that? It sounds like a decent goal.

The problem is that it's not my job to be profound. That's the work of the Holy Spirit. My job is to steward the creative gifts I've been given, develop them, share them generously, be grateful for them, but not build a totem to the words or to me. I'm just a beggar leading other beggars to the bread. So are you.

Paul wrote in First Corinthians 2:4, "When I talked with you or preached, I didn't try to prove anything by sounding wise. I simply let God's Spirit show his power" (CEV).

In a culture where pride and arrogance are highly prized commodities, it's easy for them to slip in under the radar and masquerade as "bold initiative" or "visionary leadership" or some other worthy character trait. It requires constant vigilance and reflection on our motives and how much we're trying to dictate outcomes in order to "position" ourselves.

On the job, how do you treat subordinates? How generously do you recognize and reward the efforts of others? How well do you take direction from those above you? Do you exaggerate your accomplishments and downplay mistakes? Do you play the blame game? Can you enthusiastically support someone else's ideas? In relationships, can you say, "I'm sorry. I was wrong"? Can you accept help when it's offered? Are you open to advice?

God loves to see us succeed. He's not against achievement or success or recognition for a job well done. The test is whether you know how you got there and how are you going to act once you've arrived. Can you live with walking alongside others rather than needing them to be beneath you?

Every talent we have—every ounce of intelligence, every bit of perceptiveness, initiative, wisdom and creativity—all come from God. We may have worked hard to develop them, but we didn't pay for them. They were a gift. We can be grateful for them, but we don't own them.

Second Corinthians 10:17-18 says, " 'Let him who boasts boast in the Lord.' For it is not the one who commends himself who is approved, but the one whom the Lord commends."

Oswald Chambers put it more bluntly. "Beware of posing as a profound person. God became a baby."[1]

Reality

☐ Are you clear about the difference between healthy self-confidence and pride and arrogance?

☐ Where are you most vulnerable to pride?

☐ Is it more important for you to be impressive than to admit your brokenness?

☐ If it's inappropriate to show your vulnerability in your workplace position, are you willing to share your weaknesses and limitations within your spiritual community?

When Life Hits Back

T wo weeks before Christmas I received a phone call from a shell-shocked friend, a consultant with one of the nation's Big Five management consulting firms. She was calling from another city where she was meeting with a client. She had called the office to pick up messages and learned from a coworker that the company had laid off 500 people by e-mail. She thought her job was secure, but now she wasn't so sure.

Employers certainly have the right to adjust their labor force to changing needs. It's the speed, severity and seeming caprice of today's downsizings that leaves workers gasping.

New studies show that those who lose their jobs aren't the only casualties. Employees left behind are deeply affected. They report feeling angry, disillusioned and unable to trust their employer. Their fear reduces productivity, increases the attrition rate and destroys loyalty. There's even a phrase now to describe workplace anger. We say someone has "gone postal"—a tragic reference to the disgruntled postal worker who shot his supervisor following a layoff.

Downsizing is not the only disillusioning reality about today's business environment. Every workplace has the colleague who challenges you at every turn and/or a boss who passes over you when handing out promotions. You're set up to fail on a project because of impossible deadlines and unrealistic outcomes, but your department head wanted the numbers to look good for the management team.

As Job said to God when "unfair" calamities were visited on him, "What have I done to you, O watcher of men? Why have you made me your target?" (Job 7:20). If God's in charge, why does He let "them" get away with it? Whose side is He on, anyway?

Jacob is another Bible figure who felt major disappointment when his uncle, Laban, reneged on a deal to gain the hand of Laban's daughter, Rachel (Genesis 29). Jacob was madly in love with Rachel. He agreed to work for Laban seven years without pay in return for the right to marry her. Laban agreed. When it came time for Laban to uphold his end of the deal, he pulled a bait-and-switch and gave Jacob Rachel's older sister, Leah, instead. Jacob wasn't in love with Leah. She wasn't part of the deal.

"Too bad," Laban said (my paraphrase). "Around here we do things differently. The older sister has to get married first. If you're willing to work another seven years for nothing, you can have Rachel too."

Jacob had done his part. He played by the rules. His boss changed the rules in midstream. It wasn't right. Where was God?

The question implies God's job is to spare us from trouble. But Jesus told us the truth about trouble in John

16:33: "In this world you *will have* trouble. But take heart! I have overcome the world" (emphasis added).

More than once I've prayed, "OK, Jesus. I understand the 'trouble' part. And I like the 'overcoming' plan. But could I see a little of that overcoming part right now? Now would be an especially good time."

The Bible doesn't talk nearly as much about *when* God will act as it does about *what* He will do and what our attitude is supposed to be in the meantime. "Do not fret because of evil men or be envious of those who do wrong; for like the grass they will soon wither, like green plants they will soon die away" (Psalm 37:1-2). The psalmist's point is plain. Life's not fair. Deal with it. And God will deal with it too, in time.

We learn a lot about ourselves when life lets us down. There's nothing like having your back against the wall to get your undivided attention. We see things we couldn't see before. A careless tongue. A critical spirit. Jealousy toward those for whom life is easier. Stuffed-down anger toward those who don't understand our pain. Unfair circumstances become a living laboratory where God can roll up His sleeves, get in the trenches with us and do a deep work in our heart.

God is no vague deity who posts a "Thought for the Day" in some heavenly chat room and disappears. He is *God with us* every moment we draw breath.

Furthermore, Paul promises in Second Thessalonians 1:6-7 that our disappointment will not be ignored. God will make right the current wrongs against us when Jesus returns. "God is just. He will pay back trouble to those who trouble you and give relief to you who are troubled, and to us as well."

God—in the foxhole with us today, executing justice for us in the future. The workplace need not disappoint us anymore.

Reality

- [ ] Are there currently situations in your life where you feel treated unfairly? How have you responded to them?

- [ ] When do you learn and grow the most—when things are running smoothly or when your back is against the wall?

- [ ] What have you learned about life from your major disappointments?

- [ ] How has it altered your relationship with God?

- [ ] Talk to God about what still hurts. Ask Him to make clear what He wants you to "take away" from those experiences.

- [ ] What spiritual truth will help you cope better with disappointment in the future?

Still Hazy after All These Years

I thought it was a joke when the story crossed the wires in the newsroom. A Los Angeles man named Larry Waters was reported drifting in controlled airspace at 11,000 feet near Los Angeles International Airport—in a lawn chair!

Larry, it seems, always wanted to fly. One day—apparently a day when Larry had way too much time on his hands—he devised a plan to make his dream a reality. He filled forty-six weather balloons with helium (the big balloons that are about four feet in diameter), tied them to his lawn chair, took his seat and "Look! Up in the sky! It's a bird! It's a plane! It's . . . Larry in his lawn chair!"

He took along a pellet gun to pop the balloons one at a time to return him to earth. But when his flying machine whooshed him two miles off the ground instead of the thirty feet he expected, the pellet gun didn't seem like such a great idea.

After his rescue by helicopter, a reporter asked Larry why he did it. He responded, "Because a man just can't sit around."

I love that story. It's a perfect analogy to what happens when we drift either in life or in our relationship with God. No one plans to drift. We start out with great plans. Then along comes a job loss, an unwanted divorce, an empty nest or an unexpected health crisis. Removal of the organizing principles around which we've built our lives leaves us untethered and disconnected. What starts out as temporarily treading water to regroup slips imperceptibly into a lifestyle of disengagement. It goes unnoticed until inertia becomes a strong undertow halting the forward momentum of our lives.

Drift is not limited to the valleys in life either. Rogers Kirven found it can happen to highly successful people in their forties and fifties who "cashed out" early and had every intention of spending more time with family and enjoying the American Dream.

Kirven, an entrepreneur in his forties who owns six companies, was *thisclose* to accepting a buy-out offer when he decided he ought to talk to friends and acquaintances who had already done what he was about to do. Call it a reality check.

He was so startled by their responses that he decided against selling his companies and continued his investigation—eventually talking to fifty people from the top one percent of American affluence. He found an extraordinarily high rate of divorce, depression and a rush to purchase expensive toys that were soon discarded out of boredom. What was now to be the point of their lives?

What was supposed to have been the ticket to a glorious future ended up creating a destructive vacuum. An undeveloped sense of personal mission and underdeveloped spiritual girders left these high-capacity people adrift. Kirven likened it to the parable in Luke 11 where the house is swept clean, but, if not refilled with the things of God, becomes a recipe for disaster (vs. 24-26).

Ephesians 5:15-16 says, "Be very careful, then, how you live—not as unwise but as wise, making the most of every opportunity because the days are evil."

"You can't manage your soul the way you manage a business," Kirven says. "You have to keep taking risks…but the risk is to become a person of character, using your gifts in service to the kingdom of God."

Think what would have happened if Jesus had not known His calling or strayed off mission. What if He had decided not to go through with the crucifixion? Could you blame Him? He had left a cushy life in heaven. Here He was on earth, schlepping from town to town with a management team (the disciples) that was not exactly "A" material. Pressing the flesh day in and day out. Constantly in demand.

He racked up some pretty impressive credentials in three short years. Fed a lot of hungry people. Healed the sick. Performed more than a few miracles. Through simple stories He showed people how to get their acts together. He took on the Establishment, fought for the underdog and endured endless criticism and slander. Did He have to do everything?

What if He had said, "Let someone else take it from here. I've worked hard. I've earned the right to coast the rest of the way." Would that have been all right with you? Would you mind losing the chance to have your sins forgiven and your eternal destiny secured because Jesus drifted? It's a scary thought.

Yes, Jesus kicked back when He needed to be refreshed. He didn't think twice about taking a time-out when there were big decisions to ponder. But He never lost interest. He didn't drop out.

That's because His life was never about *His* plans and *His* needs. It was about cooperating with His Father's plan—a staggering plan to save the entire world with one extraordinary sacrifice. ("Oh, and by the way, Son, it's You. You're the sacrifice.") Jesus didn't bail. He committed Himself all the way to the cross.

Now it's our turn to make a commitment, and Jesus doesn't sugarcoat the stakes. "Whoever finds his life will lose it, and whoever loses his life for my sake will find it" (Matthew 10:39). We don't have to die on a cross, but we *are* invited to help God accomplish His purposes here on earth and spread the good news.

To organize our lives around kingdom priorities will affect our time, money, energy, lifestyle and reputation. Why should that surprise you? Everything has a price. Drift has a price.

Christ earned the right to lay claim to us. Name one person who has loved you as lavishly. To ignore His call is to treat the cross as just another piece of wood put to unfortunate use.

Reality

☐ Are you drifting in your spiritual life?

☐ Where did you get off track?

☐ Have you been seduced by what Francis Schaeffer called "cash and comfort"? Do you have a sense of how God would want to use your life if you recommitted your time and talents to Him?

☐ Write down three things you will do in the next week that will give God the opportunity to re-ignite your heart.

Momma Always Loved You More

The best part of graduating from high school was that there would be no more tests. Don't get me wrong—I love to learn. But I'm not a good test taker. I was always more curious about things like why there had to be 100 questions on the test instead of, say, sixty-seven. I wondered what grade our teacher got in high school on *her* American History test. And, instead of memorizing the parts of the human brain, how about if we went to a hospital and asked them to show us a real brain? Then I could really get into it.

When I passed along my suggestions, my teacher would stare at me blankly, instruct me to turn over my paper when I was done and wait for the rest of the class to finish. Then she'd slip into the teachers' lounge and take two aspirin.

In college, I thought I'd finally found my niche. Spirited classroom discussions and essay questions were places I could shine. The only problem was the reading. There was a lot of reading, and I'm not a fast reader. I like to linger over a writer's words rather than tear through the required reading list which was usually the length of a telephone book.

That's why I hated David Jeffrey.

David and I were both English literature majors. He was brilliant—there's no other word for it. He was smarter before he pulled his socks on each morning than I'll be when I get to heaven and finally get the IQ I've requisitioned. The fact that he was the nicest guy you'd ever want to meet just meant I had to work that much harder to dislike him.

David set a personal goal one year to read 150 books. 150! Many of them weren't even on the required reading list. Worse yet, he did it. It made me sick. Here I thought I was finally in a learning environment where I could burst from my academic cocoon and soar . . . then David Jeffrey showed up and made the rest of us look like dolts.

I can share that story—along with admitting my childhood envy of Judy Clifford's wardrobe of fur-blend sweaters and my envy, as a newlywed, of our neighbor's beautiful patio and Weber BBQ grill—because I like to think I'm much too adult to act that immature now.

It's considerably more painful to admit recent feelings about a professional peer with whom I frequently work. She doesn't carry her share of the load on any given project but still manages to take all the credit and endears herself to superiors. I waffle between feelings of grudging envy ("How did she *do* that?"), jealousy and murder.

That's the problem with envy. It's not a stand-alone sin. It doesn't remain innocent very long. In the Bible, when envy is discussed it's often linked to unsavory companions like hatred, discord, selfish ambition, fits of rage and dissension (Galatians 5:20-21), or strife, malicious talk and evil suspicions (1 Timothy 6:4-5), or deceit, hypocrisy and slander (1 Peter 2:1). Not exactly the building blocks of a noble life.

Envy at its core believes someone else got what *we* deserved or, at the very least, something *they didn't* deserve. We get focused on believing the problem is *them* when it is really all about us.

Envy is dumb when you stop and think about it. I call it the boomerang sin. What it does to *us* is worse than what it does to others. Proverbs 14:30 says it rots us from the inside out. "A heart at peace gives life to the body, but envy rots the bones."

Envy works off the basic assumption that life is a zero sum game. If you gain, I lose. I admit that's definitely the way the world works for those whose hearts have not been transformed by the Holy Spirit. But it's not supposed to be characteristic of a Spirit-led life.

Regardless of the milieu in which we operate, Scripture makes clear that the mark of a Spirit-led life "is love, joy, peace, patience, kindness, goodness, faithfulness, gentleness and self-control" (Galatians 5:22-23). Could any list be more opposite envy and its nasty companions?

How do we bear that kind of fruit? I don't want to be told that one behavior is bad and this one is good unless someone is going to tell me how to get from Point A to Point B. Galatians 5:25-26 says, "Since we live by the Spirit, let us *keep in step with the Spirit*. Let us not become conceited, provoking and envying each other" (emphasis added). That means spending time reading the Bible, praying, attending a church where good spiritual food is dispensed—to learn how God intended life to work. It's about allowing Him to shape our attitudes, actions and behavior.

Did you ever take part in a marching band in high school? My daughter did. For four years I sat in the stands at every game as the Wildcats marching band strutted their stuff. If a band member got careless or wasn't paying attention and failed to march in step to the carefully choreographed routines, the result was painful to watch. And, if other band members fell prey to the confusion, eventually even the music itself fell apart.

Contrast that with elite bands that march at halftime on TV during college bowl games. They are a breathtaking wave of human precision. Hundreds of musicians fanning out across an enormous football field, spelling out words and creating pictures in a kaleidoscope of changing formations. The crowd roars its approval because they recognize what the band members are "saying" with their movements. The message jumps out at us because everyone is marching in step. It's beautiful to behold.

Envy messes up God's choreography for a well-lived life. And it throws off more than just you. It means misery for everyone involved, and it's not fun to watch either.

God doesn't ask me to write the music or choreograph the routine of my life. He already has a plan. There's no uniform to buy. Responsibility for winning the game is not on my shoulders. I just have to pay attention to the Director and follow His lead.

Reality

☐ Do you currently feel discontented or resentful over someone else's advantages, friendships or possessions?

☐ How has it affected your behavior? Are you happy with the result?

☐ What do you wish were true?

☐ Select one trait from the list of the fruit of the Spirit (page 27-28). Ask God to bring you in step with Him and grow that trait in your life.

The Truth about Deep Weeds

In 1998, Illinois governor James Edgar decided not to seek re-election. He left at the top of his game after a long political career as a state legislator, Secretary of State and two-term governor. As Edgar reflected on his political career, a reporter brought up the fact that the governor had lost his first bid for the Illinois House in 1974. The governor was asked how it changed his career.

"I learned two lessons. One, you can always lose. Two, I never wanted to lose again." He said people tried to console him with the fact that Abraham Lincoln, Illinois' most famous native son, lost his first election too. Edgar told them, "There are all kinds of things about Lincoln I don't want to duplicate. Lincoln got shot."[1]

Failure is something we like to talk about in hindsight, preferably after it's been overcome with subsequent success. It's as if we can safely admit failure only after we have regained the upper hand.

That's unfortunate. I think that "going to school" on our failures is the best preparation we have for handling later successes.

All failures are not equal. After the Super Bowl game one year, reporters accosted the coach of the losing team and asked him about the ramifications of the loss—not just on his career, but on professional athletics and the stock market. "Fellas," he told them, shaking his head in disbelief, "it's a football game! We'll live."

I received a "D" once in college. It sticks in my mind like a pebble stuck in my shoe. Why do I remember the grade and not the fact that it happened the semester I carried nineteen hours of credit, worked a part-time job, got engaged and spent six weeks in the college health center with mononucleosis? Putting it in perspective reduces its ability to nip at my confidence.

Serious failures are a different matter. If a marriage falls apart or a business goes belly-up, the pain goes far deeper—especially if we are culpable. We carry the shame and guilt like a dead animal draped around our neck. That's when we need to know God has not permanently turned His back on us.

God views failure differently than we do. Assuredly, we must "own" our sin and ask for His forgiveness. Not all the consequences of our sins are reversible. Nevertheless, we can hand it over to God to decide what's salvageable and stand amazed for the rest of our lives that nothing is beyond the reach of His grace.

Failure is a circumstance, not a life sentence. I have a friend who spent fifteen years in the extremely challenging restaurant industry. From the day she opened her first franchise restaurant, she felt she had a mandate from God. She was to run the business with integrity and honesty, provide excellent service, put out a quality product at a good price and champion those same values to everyone she came in contact with—employees, vendors and customers.

It was not a cakewalk. Someone threw a bomb into the restaurant three weeks after it opened. Their chief competitor opened right next door. "Every day," she says, "I gave the business back to God. It was up to Him to keep it going."

As the business flourished, her husband joined the company as chief financial officer. Fifteen years later, they owned fourteen restaurants. They were enjoying financial success, the respect of peers and the satisfaction of former employees who came back year after year to say thanks for what they had learned about integrity and work and life.

One day, the franchise company changed the rules. My friend and her husband felt they could no longer operate successfully without compromising the values they felt called to model. The parting of ways was messy and exacted a heavy emotional and financial toll. It was not the outcome they expected. To observers it looked like a colossal failure.

I wish failures didn't have to be in plain view—especially in view of those who hold biblical values in low regard. My friend admits it was a painful time. She and her husband revisited what happened over and over again in order to drain off the wisdom and the truths from the situation before discarding the rest.

Now she's able to convincingly talk about the whole experience as a "Romans 8:28 thing": "And we know that in all things God works for the good of those who love him, who have been called according to his purpose." She says she'd do it all over again but would do a few things differently. Friendships and personal needs were neglected; she won't let that happen again.

"God hands you a package, and you open it," she says. "You don't always know what's inside. I want to be expended doing whatever He gives me to do." Today she's a successful executive coach who counsels other CEOs about how to manage their businesses and their lives.

Jesus' death on the cross looked like a failure. He hung there exposed and forsaken by His own Father. An angry mob called Him a phony. He warned His disciples it was coming, but when it happened I doubt they believed any part of it could remotely "work for the good of those who love Him." Who knew?

That's the point, really. In the midst of what looks like colossal failure—real or imagined, large or small, our fault or someone else's—God's perspective is the one that counts, regardless of other, louder voices. He says the good guys win in the end—and He ought to know.

Our job is to do what He told us to do until He gets back.

Reality

☐ How do you look at failure?

☐ Are you able to talk about your failures as well as your successes?

☐ What have they taught you about yourself?

☐ Are you able to let go of past mistakes, confess your part to God and move on?

☐ Are you stuck on any past situation?

☐ What do you need to do to address it?

☐ How are you a different person as a result of those experiences?

Let's Not Go There

J've never met a person who is not afraid of something. Even people we call "fearless" are typically brave in a particular setting, not necessarily in their whole life. I once heard about a man who made his living putting his head into the mouths of lions at the circus, but he feared flying in an airplane.

Fear doesn't care how old we are or how much power we have. Like a perfectly targeted spear, it goes right for the chinks in our particular armor. It doesn't have to be a big opening. It just has to hit us where we feel most vulnerable.

Wealthy people have more resources to combat their fears, but they are not immune. On December 3, 1999, one of the world's wealthiest and most influential bankers, billionaire Edmond Safra, died in a fire in his own lavish apartment in the tiny principality of Monaco. Safra was not a man obsessed with losing his money. Rather, he feared for his personal safety.

According to one published account, Safra traveled with a dozen bodyguards, many of them former Israeli commandos. The building in which he lived boasted an impenetrable security system. When he married, the prenuptial agreement reportedly ran 600 pages—presumably to protect him from any conceivable eventuality. He was a man using the full resources at his command to manage his fear of personal harm.[1]

In the midst of all these safeguards, investigators say that a male nurse, in a fit of pique at another on-site nurse, started a fire in Safra's apartment. The two nurses were locked in a power struggle over who would be Safra's chief caregiver, a position that paid slightly more money than other staff positions.

When the fire broke out, Safra's wife called him on a cell phone from another part of the vast apartment, urging him to flee. He thought it was a trick and that the fire was a diversion to get him out of the apartment. He refused to leave, and he perished in the fire. Despite all his elaborate security, the raging fear in his head is what ultimately killed him.

I'm quite adept at creating my own poor man's version of an impenetrable security system when I feel threatened. It's a barricaded heart, a facade of bravado that says, "I have it all together." While less exotic (and certainly less expensive) than Edmund Safra's security system, it's equally absurd.

It never works. In the end, just like Safra, I don't feel any safer—just lonely and cut off. Courageous people who are fully alive don't live their lives sequestered behind walls—visible or invisible.

God's Word offers plentiful reassurance when fear has us in its grip and suggests there's a better way to feel safe:

> Say to those with fearful hearts,
>   "Be strong, do not fear;
> your God will come,
>   he will come with vengeance;
> with divine retribution
>   he will come to save you." (Isaiah 35:4)

> The LORD is my light and my salvation—
>   whom shall I fear?
> The LORD is the stronghold of my life—
>   of whom shall I be afraid? . . .
> For in the day of trouble
>   he will keep me safe in his dwelling;
> he will hide me in the shelter of his tabernacle.
>   (Psalm 27:1, 5)

Fear is on the loose in the world, but it slinks away when it comes face-to-face with faith. It means we must intentionally choose to align ourselves with God's point of view, even if our feelings aren't quite on board yet. It's acting "as if" God will do what He promised, even when our "truster" has been damaged and when counting on Him feels like the scariest thing we've ever done.

God wants me to be something I have never been. To accomplish that end, He will take me where I've never gone.

He'll ask me to walk right up to my fears and tell them to back off because God and I are coming through.

When we push past the fear and throw our arms around God, a remarkable thing happens. Fear shrinks down to size, and faith starts calling the shots. It's the moment God has been waiting for. We are finally free to learn firsthand that God is the most extraordinary security system in the world.

Reality

☐ What are you most afraid of?

☐ When was the last time you experienced God's protection?

☐ If you have not felt aware of God's protection, why do you think that is? Ask God for insight about it.

☐ What coping mechanisms do you use to feel safe instead of trusting God?

☐ What would make it possible for you to turn to Him more often?

Caught in the Act of Being Yourself

he first beat I covered as a radio news reporter in Chicago was criminal court. The aging Cook County Criminal Court Building at 26th and California sat in a blighted south-side neighborhood like a great stone sphinx. A steady stream of innocent people, mopes and lowlifes passed through its doors to stand toe-to-toe with the criminal justice system. After two years on the beat, I got the feeling everyone was either working an angle or trying to be something he was not.

Nowhere was this more evident than at the trial of mass-murderer John Wayne Gacy. For months the public carried in their minds a mental image of Gacy as he appeared in the mug shot taken on the day of his arrest. Hundreds of times in print and on television we saw the same shot of a puffy-faced, unshaven man with a menacing scowl and messy hair. He definitely looked like someone capable of killing thirty-three people—twenty-nine of whom he buried in the crawl space under his house.

That's probably why the spectators, assembled in the courtroom the first day of trial, let out a collective gasp when Gacy appeared. In walked a clean-shaven, well-groomed jovial man, twenty to thirty pounds lighter, wearing a three-piece suit. He could have passed for a favorite uncle—the one who pulls your kids onto his lap to read *The Little Engine That Could*. Gacy's metamorphosis was downright creepy.

Identity is a tricky thing. We know intellectually that appearance is not the most important part of our identity, but at times it sure seems more important than whatever is in second place. We pigeonhole people by their wrappers.

I experienced firsthand how style can trump substance when a TV news director encouraged me to switch from radio news to television news. Matter-of-factly, he described how I'd be expected to wear my hair, the weight I would need to be and the restrictions on my wardrobe. When I realized this new-and-improved person he described bore no resemblance to the real me and had little to do with journalism, I took a pass. I didn't like the idea of having my appearance determined by a stranger and vetted by other strangers with remote controls.

Genesis 27 reports the first case of counterfeit identity. Jacob went to elaborate lengths to assume the identity of his older brother, Esau. Jacob wanted his close-to-death, almost-blind father, Isaac, to bestow the blessing reserved for the oldest son on him instead of his twin.

Jacob prepared the special meal his dad had requested of Esau, dressed up in his brother's clothes and went so far as to cover his hands and neck with goatskins to replicate his brother's hairiness. When Dad got suspicious, Jacob took the scam to the limit and flat-out lied, claiming to be Esau.

Strictly speaking, Jacob stole Esau's blessing, not his identity—as if that made his deceit less reprehensible. But his troubles stemmed from wanting what was not his—something reserved for someone else—and not valuing who God made him to be.

I've never stolen someone's birthright or blessing, but I've taken on jobs and roles that were someone else's idea of what constituted a worthwhile life for me. Often it wasn't the life God intended. I wasn't trying to be deceitful. I didn't know who *I* was. When others delivered up their well-meaning "shoulds" and "oughts," I thought it showed openness and teachability on my part to assume the identity and roles offered.

Another faulty notion is to believe our job forms the basis of our identity. A job is a role. It's not who we are. If we define ourselves by our job, what happens when the job goes away? That's why people fall apart over a job loss.

I didn't understand that God has a blessing for each one of us that's much bigger than any job or role. It's a custom-made identity that no one else gets. There are clues to it in our personality, in what we're passionate about and in our unique combination of gifts and talents.

FaithWorks, the Dallas-based initiative that grew out of Bob Buford's book, *Halftime*, challenges business people to move from an identity based on success to an identity based on kingdom significance.

Entrepreneurs, executives and other professionals dig deep to explore together how God made them. They're asked, "What makes you laugh? What makes you cry? What are you willing to sleep on the floor for?"

Once they've gained an understanding of their God-given identity, they are given the opportunity to partner with ministries and other non-profit ventures that make a good match to their profile. It's not a job. It's about living as who God made them to be, to promote God's values to a needy world.

And what happened to Jacob? His deceit in counterfeiting Esau's identity previewed a life that left a trail of tears. He learned the hard way that a stolen blessing is no blessing at all. He needed a blessing of his own.

Finally, one night when he was alone, defeated and fearing for his life, Jacob wrestled with God. He needed to find the life with *his* name on it. God gave him a new name and a chance to start over.

For the rest of Jacob's life, he carried a visible reminder of his God-encounter—he walked with a limp. But the next day, he reconciled with his estranged brother, and his life took a whole new direction.

I trust people who walk with a limp more than those who strut. They've learned the hard way the truth of Acts 17:27-28: "He isn't far from any of us, and he gives us the power to live, to move, and to be who we are" (CEV).

It can be painful to wrestle with God and face the truth about who we are and who we are not. A lot of what we see isn't good—which explains why we never wanted to look in the first place. But our God is the God of Second Chances. He gives us a new name—"Forgiven." It's never too late to find out who we were supposed to be all along.

Reality

☐ Do you have a clear sense of the identity God gave you, or are you living out the expectations of others?

☐ Have you confused your job or one of your roles (parent, child, volunteer, neighbor) with your identity?

☐ What part of your personal makeup most puzzles you?

☐ Are you afraid God might have an identity for you which you don't want? Wrestle with God about this.

You're OK—
I'm a Mess

hen *Peanuts* creator Charles Schulz died, 355 million readers in seventy-five countries mourned the loss of the man who every day for nearly fifty years put into words their own insecurities. Schulz often said the angst expressed by the hapless Charlie Brown, the irrepressible Lucy, Schroeder, Snoopy and the rest of the *Peanuts* gang came from his own life experience.

"I was a bland, stupid-looking kid who started off badly and failed everything," Schulz once said.[1] When he returned home from World War II, he fell in love with a woman who, despite their long courtship, turned down his proposal of marriage. It was another rejection which affected him for years.

Schulz was a committed Christian and devoted family man. He enjoyed the wealth and fame that came with creating the most widely syndicated comic strip is history. Yet it was widely reported that he struggled his entire life with insecurity, melancholy, depression and panic attacks.

There is nothing quite as debilitating as not being sure whether you measure up. As a male friend once said to me, "It's more acceptable in this country to be physically handicapped than to struggle with self-worth, but I'm not sure which is the more devastating. Men struggle with it as much as women. We just do a better job of hiding it."

From arrogance at one extreme to social withdrawal on the other, insecurity wears many guises. We've all known work associates who have more faces than Crayola has colors. Were they being politically savvy by never taking an unpopular stance even when it was called for? Or were they just too insecure to disturb the status quo? Secure people can risk being unloved. They know it'll happen anyway.

The Artful Dodger type of insecurity deflects compliments and dreads moving up the ladder for fear of being found out as a fraud. People may work long hours not because they have to but because they're not sure their normal day's work is worth the same as their colleagues'. If anything good starts coming their way, they figure they must be in the wrong lane looking at oncoming traffic.

That was Moses' story when God showed up and told him to go to Pharaoh and secure the release of all the Israelites. *Oh, sure*, Moses probably thought to himself. *Like Pharaoh can't wait for me to take his entire pool of slave labor off his hands. And have you forgotten about that Egyptian I murdered? Why do you think I've been hiding out way down here in Midian for forty years?*

"Who am I, that I should go to Pharaoh and bring the Is-raelites out of Egypt?" Moses asked God in Exodus 3:11. More excuses followed (author paraphrases): "What if they ask who sent me?" (3:13), "What if they don't listen or believe me?" (4:1), "What about the fact that I'm a lousy speaker?" (4:10), "There must be some mistake, God. You can't be serious that You want *me*."

It doesn't matter if you're a secretary who gets the chance to be an assistant account executive or if you're the president of a company whose stakeholders want you to take them public in a market already flooded with IPOs. There will be times in life when you come up to a line in the sand where your supply of confidence ends and something within you says, *Uh oh. This is as far as I go.*

That's when you have to decide whose truth you are go-ing to believe. Will you believe the earthly father who told you that you wouldn't amount to anything and whom you've subconsciously been trying to please ever since? Will it be the boss who said you weren't management material because you don't have an MBA? Maybe you've decided it's God who has disqualified you because of past sins. You're certain He sees you as one of the models of the human race that didn't quite turn out, dismissed as a major disappoint-ment.

Romans 9:20-21 says, "But who are you, O man, to talk back to God? 'Shall what is formed say to Him who formed it, "Why did you make me like this?"' Does not the potter have the right to make out of the same lump of clay some pottery for noble purposes and some for common use?"

God does not downsize His plans to fit our insecurities, but *we* can downsize what He is able to do *in us* by how we view ourselves.

Romans 12:4 in the J.B. Phillips translation says, "Try to have a sane estimate of your capabilities by the light of the faith that God has given to you all." A healthy self-worth means understanding that there is no perfect set of talents and traits. Our accomplishments do not have to be inflated or diminished. Our failures are not denied, but we don't need to dwell on them.

When God describes the creation of Adam and Eve He doesn't say whether Adam was a great athlete or handsome hunk. He doesn't say if Eve was a natural blond with a great figure and a knockout sense of humor. I think He did that on purpose so we wouldn't constantly compare ourselves to the perfect man and woman. (Oh, if I had only been 5'7" like Eve. . . .)

We *are* told, however, that we're made in God's image, and that He thought what He made was good . . . *very* good (Genesis 1:25, 31).

When God instilled in your DNA all that makes you *you*, He didn't have a backup person to play your part if you bailed. There's no understudy to take over being Verla if I don't want to be me. He needs me to be fully me.

The same goes for you. He's hoping we'll agree with Him—that how He made us is good . . . very good.

When Dr. Joseph Stowell became president of Moody Bible Institute following a long tenure by his beloved predecessor, Dr. George Sweeting, person after person stopped Stowell in the halls to say, "Well, Joe, you've got big shoes to fill."

Stowell finally replied, "I know. They're too big for me to fill. That's why I brought my own."

Reality

☐ How would you rate your self-esteem?

☐ Who has had the biggest influence on your sense of self-worth? Was it positive or negative? How does it affect your life today?

☐ Are there lies you've believed about your value as a human being? Name them and ask God to change your mind.

☐ What is something about yourself you can celebrate today?

Attack of the Performance Police

hilip Yancey blew my cover when he wrote *What's So Amazing About Grace?* Until then I thought I'd done a pretty good job of believing perfectionism had a place in the Christian life.

Oh, sure, there's all that talk in the Bible about the grace God extends to forgive my sins and save me from an eternity without Him. It was the other grace that confused me—the everyday grace. What was that all about? It sounded simple enough. Turn to God when you mess up, take the grace that sets things straight, get over yourself, move on. It was too . . . well . . . perfect. God's system didn't *need* me and all my effort. How could I score points with God if I didn't have a chance to show Him what a good job I could do?

I hate to admit it, but I acted for years like once the salvation question was addressed, it was all mastery from there. Read the right books on discipleship, listen to tapes, memorize the right verses and whip through a few Bible studies. Like boning up for your ACT or GSAT exam. Grace would be there if I needed it. But, hey, if I were devoted and disciplined, I wouldn't need it that often, right?

In America, performance rules! Everywhere we turn, someone is measuring, evaluating and ranking us to see if we pass muster. Educators determine our intelligence and acquired knowledge based on our test scores. Economists tell us whether we are lower class, middle class or upper class based on our earnings. Personal trainers evaluate our fitness by the number of sit-ups we can execute and how many pounds we can benchpress.

The implied message is, "Get your act together. And if you don't have it together, keep quiet about it." (Remember the ad slogan, "Never let them see you sweat?")

But Philip Yancey says (and he got the idea from God), "Grace is not about finishing last or first; it is about not counting."[1]

Not keep score? Do you think I'm doing all these spiritual push-ups for my health?

I remember the time my car slid on an oil puddle as I slowed to a stop at a traffic light. The car lost traction, and I slid into the car in front of me. I tapped it so lightly I wasn't surprised that neither car showed signs of damage. The other driver and I laughed it off, and I drove away.

The next day, however, my entire front bumper popped neatly in half. Apparently I had hit a fault line in the fiberglass frame.

The manager of a local body shop explained that my "precision driving" would cost me about $400. Disgusted, I took the estimate, got back into my car, threw the car in reverse without looking and rammed into a telephone pole (a pole I'm sure was erected while I was inside getting my estimate).

Sheepishly, I re-entered the body shop and asked for an estimate for a bumper.

"I just gave it to you!" the owner said, with more than a trace of irritation.

"Uh . . . not that bumper," I said.

Caught in the act of being human. I hate it when that happens.

That's why I appreciate the apostle Paul. Paul had the kind of impressive credentials that would make a run-of-the-mill Pharisee weep. But there was no confusion in his mind about needing a lot of grace. He was OK with that. In fact, he made weakness a rallying cry.

In First Timothy 1:15-16, he told his young assistant,

> Here is a trustworthy saying that deserves full acceptance: [In other words, listen up, Timothy, this is one of the most important things you'll ever hear me say.]: Christ Jesus came into the world to save sinners—of whom I am the worst. But for that very reason I was shown mercy, so that in me, the worst of sinners, Christ Jesus might display his unlimited pa-

tience as an example for those who would believe on him and receive eternal life.

Ahhhh . . . at last there's something I can do perfectly. I
can embrace that I'm human and stop denying Christ the
opportunity to demonstrate His grace.

Let the weakness begin!

Reality

☐ Are you performance-driven?

☐ Do you still want to live with that orientation?

☐ Are you able to accept your mistakes and weaknesses?

☐ Are you willing to ask for help when you need it?

☐ What has been the price of your perfectionism if
this is an issue for you?

☐ What is the first area of your life where you'd
like to try a different approach?

☐ Write a short note to yourself committing to cut
yourself some slack and take more advantage of
God's grace.

Visions of a Different Life

There are two kinds of letters people never forget—love letters and letters that start out, "We regret to inform you. . . . " Love letters bring good news. Regret letters alert us that we're about to lose something. While the pain of loss eventually subsides, regrets can whisper in our ears indefinitely, filling our minds with endless "if-onlys" and "might-have-beens" that can lead to a postponed life.

In 1983, when America Online executive Ted Leonsis thought he was about to die in a plane crash, he started writing down 101 things he would do if he survived. If he lived, he wanted to face death the next time with a minimum of regrets. So far, he's checked off nearly two-thirds of the items on his list and plans to have the list distributed at his funeral.[1]

Not all regrets are as easily redeemed. We don't always get a do-over. In *A Grace Disguised*, Gerald Sittser describes the loss of his mother, wife and daughter in one catastrophic car accident caused by a drunk driver. There would be no tomorrow to make right his yesterday. "Regret is especially bitter," Sittser says, "because we are deprived of the very context—relationship, job or whatever—that is needed to reverse the failure and set a new course before it is too late."

He argues persuasively for dealing with our regrets to avoid living in a perpetual state of guilt. "We think there is no forgiveness or redemption because we are deprived of the opportunity to right our wrongs." But, he says, "Regret can lead to transformation if we view loss as an opportunity to take inventory of our lives."[2]

Think about the losses in your life. Set aside, for the moment, the irreplaceable losses—like the death of a loved one—that are in a league all their own. Think about the losses, especially related to job or career, that may not scream for immediate attention but gnaw away at your peace of mind. Do you carry regrets about

- choices you've made?
- opportunities lost, roads not taken?
- playing it safe and not taking more risks?
- speaking inappropriately or not speaking when you should have?
- trying to prove something to people who didn't care?

- thinking you knew better?

- caring too much about money, title, recognition, comfort or security?

- not leaving sooner or not staying longer?

- neglecting family or friends or your own needs?

- betraying a colleague?

- belittling a subordinate?

- not playing fair?

- letting other people drive your decisions?

- the time you devoted to your work at the expense of your personal life?

- not trusting your instincts?

- not trusting others?

- not believing in yourself?

Regrets represent the deepest sighs of our soul. They're like tiny weights that invisibly latch onto our spirits, slowing our forward momentum. Revisiting the regrets, naming them, owning any part we played in them and asking God's forgiveness cut us loose from the weights so we can soar again.

Romans 8:1 says, "Therefore, there is now no condemnation for those who are in Christ Jesus." The past may not have been pretty, but it's over. We are redeemed from the woulda-coulda-shouldas of our regrets.

I'll bet Paul had plenty of regrets when he first became a Christian. He hunted down Christians before he was converted. He is widely believed to have given his approval of the fatal stoning of Stephen. But Paul knew he couldn't change the past. He let it go. God's grace and forgiveness released him from a mountain of regret.

"Forgetting what is behind and straining toward what is ahead," Paul said, "I press on toward the goal to win the prize for which God has called me heavenward in Christ Jesus" (Philippians 3:13-14).

You can't step in the same river twice. Life flows on. You can stand in the stream, wishing things were different, or you can let Christ take you the rest of the way on a current of grace.

Reality

- ☐ What can be said of you today that wasn't true ten years ago?

- ☐ Have regrets robbed you? What have they taken?

- ☐ How would you be living differently if you had no regrets?

- ☐ What would you like people to say about you at your funeral that they wouldn't be able to say now?

- ☐ Write down steps you can take to make it a reality.

How We Got That Way

The sophistication of products and services in today's marketplace means that jobs are more
complicated than ever. Training is critical. But a
company's workforce may stretch around the globe. That
means the traditional corporate training model (a teacher
in a classroom, a manual and a lecture format) isn't always
an option. Sophisticated interactive computer-based training has stepped in to fill the void.

I had the opportunity once to observe a company working on the cutting edge of this revolution in corporate
training. They created software that simulated real-life situations an employee would face on the job. It allowed employees to "practice" how to handle hundreds of situations
and take chances without suffering real-world consequences.

If they made a mistake, the software automatically re-
trieved videotaped comments and suggestions from real-

life coaches who, at one time, had done what the employees were learning to do. They acted as sort of mentors-in-a-box. The idea was for the employee to learn from someone else's past mistake and, ideally, not repeat it.

There was also customized software that captured a company's history in a video storytelling format. War stories, insights and lessons learned were catalogued in hundreds of video vignettes that covered every conceivable situation an employee might face.

When an employee ran into a problem, he or she could access the company's historical memory bank and draw from the company's wealth of accumulated wisdom. Their aided "remembering" was one more way to assure their future success.

The past plays an equally powerful role in our personal lives in shaping who we are, how we act and what we will do in the future. The question is, "Are we making the most of our memories?"

The past often gets a bum rap. Typically, the first things we remember are mistakes or unpleasant memories. It's hard to get past the pain to what those experiences can teach us.

Reviewing past mistakes, however, can go a long way toward preventing the repetition of destructive behavior. Remembering past successes can give us courage to face future challenges. And sweet memories can act as a balm on a hurting heart when current joy is in short supply.

I have an adult daughter with whom I enjoy a special bond. During her teen years, when I felt particularly inept as a parent, I took great comfort in remembering something that happened when she was in the third grade.

Her teacher had instituted a reward system whereby kids could earn points all semester for a variety of good deeds and model behavior. The last day of the semester, the teacher held an auction where the kids could bid on items using the points they had accumulated.

The kids and their parents donated books, trinkets and toys they didn't want anymore to the auction, like a white elephant sale. As the stash in the prize closet grew, the kids' anticipation grew along with it. Auction Day was seen as only slightly less thrilling than Christmas.

Lisa had worked very hard to accumulate one of the highest point totals in her class. She didn't share with me which prizes she had her eyes on. All I knew was she barely slept the night before the auction, worrying that someone else would take what she wanted.

The next day, after school, I met the bus, eager to help her carry what I expected would be quite a hoard of goodies. The kids got off the bus in high spirits, laden with their treasures. Lisa stepped off the bus, grinning from ear to ear, proudly carrying a small homemade wooden jewelry box. It had taken every point she'd earned to buy it. It was for me.

I still have that box. I can't bear to part with it. Maybe someday I'll give it to one of her daughters when she starts her own family. I'll tell my granddaughter about Lisa's love for her own imperfect mom and ask her to give Lisa the same grace. It's worth remembering.

God is big on remembering. In the Old Testament, God often instructed the children of Israel to remember and celebrate examples of His faithfulness and deliverance. He knew the power of remembrance to carry us through present difficulties and brace us for obstacles up ahead.

In the book of Joshua, Moses' successor led the children of Israel through an exhausting marathon of battles on their way to claim the Promised Land. At each important juncture, Joshua, at God's instruction, erected a monument so they would remember what happened in those places.

When God parted the waters of the Jordan River so the children of Israel could cross over, just as He had done with the parting of the Red Sea, Joshua made a monument from the stones in the riverbed and said,

> In the future, when your descendants ask their fathers, "What do these stones mean?" tell them, "Israel crossed the Jordan on dry ground. . . . The LORD your God did to the Jordan just what he had done to the Red Sea . . . so that all the peoples of the earth might know that the hand of the LORD is powerful and so that you might always fear the LORD your God." (Joshua 4:21-24)

Have you mined your past for all it has to teach you? When you think about the bosses and jobs you've had and the places you've worked, do you think about the fact that God was there with you in all of it, even the times it felt like He had abandoned you?

The two of you—you and God—have a remarkable shared history. Take advantage of His willingness to revisit it with you and teach you from it. Like those mentors-in-a-box, He can put your past in a whole new light. And He doesn't need a computer to do it.

Reality

- [ ] What are the first memories that come to mind when you think about your past?

- [ ] Have you made certain experiences off-limits to remembering?

- [ ] Is it time to revisit them with God?

- [ ] What have you learned about yourself from past work experiences?

- [ ] How do those memories affect your actions today?

- [ ] How should they affect you?

- [ ] Talk to God about what is hard for you about re-membering.

Hiding Our Junk

As a business consultant I hear a lot of company "secrets." It may involve information about a new product launch, a potential merger or, more often, a crisis that's brewing. I sign a confidentiality agreement promising not to divulge what I'm about to learn. Secrets are serious business.

The only time I ever found a secret "amusing" was when I interviewed the director of the National Archives in Washington, D.C. The courtly gentleman looked like he'd spent most of his life lost in library stacks collecting names and dates off public records. But, oh, did he have stories to tell about people who used the National Archives to trace their genealogy and who discovered unwanted family secrets along the way.

He described one wealthy dowager who hired a professional genealogist to write a narrative of her family history. Unfortunately, the researcher found one of the woman's ancestors had been a brutal criminal who died in the electric chair at Sing Sing Prison in New York.

The woman begged the genealogist to expunge the criminal from the family tree, but he refused. Finally, they worked out a compromise. The researcher wrote that her relative "occupied the Chair of Applied Electricity at a prominent eastern institution." The guy definitely has a future in public relations.

Secrets are pieces of our lives we conceal because they don't fit the other parts of our lives. We know—without asking—that bringing them out in the open would make major waves. Why else would we hide them?

"No one would understand," we say. "The fallout would be too much," as if secrets don't carry their own consequences.

What if airplane maintenance crews serviced only three of an airplane's four engines because the fourth engine was hidden and out of reach? The plane might be able to fly for awhile, but it would never function at its full potential; its capacity would be diminished, and the long-term risks of disaster would be above average.

About the only thing that thrives in a dark, hidden environment is mushrooms. All the good stuff lives in the light. On a personal level, the parts of ourselves we hide are cut off from love, truth, honesty and wholeness that can only be found out in the open.

The Bible encourages us to leave darkness behind and move into the light.

- "So let us put aside the deeds of darkness and put on the armor of light." (Romans 13:12)

- "For you were once darkness, but now you are light in the Lord. Live as children of light." (Ephesians 5:8)

- "You have set our iniquities before you, our secret sins in the light of your presence." (Psalm 90:8)

I spent years worrying about the consequences of exposing my secrets to the light. I should have spent more time understanding what happens when you protect the darkness—I would have acted sooner. Secrets are not benign.

I had a magnificent jade plant for fifteen years. It was huge compared to most jades. Its limbs held hundreds of exotic waxy leaves. One day without warning, its main stem split in half, revealing massive root rot. One side completely broke off. The other side was too lopsided to stand on its own, and it too quickly died. The plant showed no outward sign of what was taking place inside until it was too late to do anything about it. Sometimes the weight of our secrets can break us when we least expect it.

There's a street ministry in Chicago that reaches out to male prostitutes with the love of Christ. It's a tough ministry. Many of the "regulars" on the street are men who dropped out of school and left home at an early age to escape intolerable family situations. Without an education, they can't get a job, so they turn to the street to support themselves. The shame of what they do under cover of darkness fuels other addictions to numb their loss of self-respect. The inner darkness keeps getting bigger until whatever light is left is pretty dim. It either slowly kills them, or they decide to move toward the light. It's a battle.

An Emmaus Ministries staff worker asked one young man who chose to face his problems and go into treatment what the turning point was in his decision. The man confided he was tired of brushing his teeth in the shower. Puzzled, the staff worker asked him to explain.

"I never thought I'd get so low in life that I'd do what I did out on the street," he explained. "I brush my teeth in the shower because I just can't stand to look at myself in the mirror anymore."

Bringing our junk out into the open doesn't mean the whole world has to know. It means finding a safe place and safe people with whom to share the truth so we can reclaim the parts of us that have been lost to the darkness. It's about getting our lives back.

Secrets are uncomfortable to talk about. They make us squirm and listening to other people's secrets feels like meddling. I've lived both with them and without them. I've learned that living in the light can save your life.

God can see in the dark. The rest of us stumble around and get hurt. Do yourself a favor. Turn on the Light.

☐ What have you kept hidden from the people who are closest to you?

☐ How do you feel about yourself because of your "withholds"?

☐ What would be the consequence of bringing this information to light?

☐ What are the consequences of keeping it hidden?

☐ Do you have a mature, grace-filled Christian friend, pastor or counselor with whom you can share your secrets?

☐ Ask God to direct you to the right person. Talk to Him about your fears.

He Who Hesitates
. . . Is Toast

I don't know any Christian who says, "I think I'll let myself be seduced today." But it happens. A coworker brushes up against you while exiting an elevator, and it physically registers as something more. You go out to dinner with the boss after a big client "win," and the conversation subtly turns personal. A longtime family friend starts giving you extra attention, and it feels good. Exhaustion—the enemy of genuine love—leaves you longing for the comfort of intimacy but without the energy to invest in the real thing.

In the midst of these inklings, Satan slinks around speaking in his native tongue—lying—about how "it's no big deal." Or *Hey, he didn't mean anything by that. Don't be so prudish.* Or *You can handle this. You know the limits.* Or *What's the harm in an innocent flirtation? No one is getting hurt.* Unfulfilled longings make us easy prey.

It's the Garden of Eden all over again. Thinking we know best. Believing we can handle it.

When I was in junior high, I had a quarter horse named Rex. Rex was a decent horse but boring compared to Dad's palomino stallion, a wild and beautiful beast. One time, I went to the stable where both horses were boarded and convinced the stablehand that my dad had given me permission to ride his horse (a flat-out lie, since I was strictly forbidden to do so).

I took off on the horse across an open meadow at a breezy pace, confident I could handle him. Within seconds, he bolted into a blazing gallop. His terrifying speed put him firmly in control and left me hanging on for dear life.

A fence loomed in the distance. He galloped to within five feet of it, stopped on a dime and catapulted me twenty feet over it. I landed, unconscious, inches from a giant boulder that could have killed me instantly.

Temptation is like that. It seems like such a good idea at the time. But the moment we entertain the notion that we can handle it, we catapult ourselves into a whole new level of risk. Satan doesn't play fair. He just needs an opening—a moment of hesitation—and he's off and running.

It isn't the temptation that's the problem. Even pure hearts get tempted. It's what we do with it. Matthew 4 recounts how Jesus was tempted three times by Satan in the wilderness. The confrontation was not over sexual issues. But if we believe Hebrews 4:15—that Jesus was tempted in every way just as we are—then the wilderness temptation will give us clues about how He may have handled other temptations.

Jesus didn't test His spiritual maturity by unnecessarily putting Himself in harm's way. He didn't entertain Satan's argument as an option. He didn't try to figure out how to have it both ways. He didn't allow His feelings to coach His actions. Immediately and unequivocally, He summoned Scripture as His defense and reality check.

Dallas Willard says if we spend enough time with God, He will bring us to a level of spiritual maturity where we don't "miss" sin. It will no longer look good. We'll know what's real and what's counterfeit. Jesus spent enough time with the Father to recognize Satan's pitiful ploy for what it was.

Temptation is a fact of life. Purity comes from turning away from temptation early on, instead of putting ourselves in harm's way when we don't have to. Ultimately, handling temptation is not just knowing right from wrong. It's spending enough time with God to eliminate the hesitation.

Reality

- ☐ Where in your life have you been kidding yourself about temptation?

- ☐ Have you been working both sides of the fence?

- ☐ What's preventing you from being unequivocal?

- ☐ Do you believe God can help you control passionate desires?

- ☐ What unfulfilled longings are behind your vulnerability to sexual temptation?

- ☐ Who is an appropriate person with whom you can discuss this?

- ☐ Set a date by which you will contact that person.

Sticks and Stones and Other Sharp Objects

J spent two years covering the political beat when I was a broadcast journalist, first based at City Hall and later at the State of Illinois Building across the street. It was a tough beat. If you wanted to do justice to the beat, you needed to know a little about government, economics, finance and law. It also helped to know where everyone's skeletons were buried. The annual budget hearings were especially onerous. I always felt that attendance at those hearings should be part of the mandatory sentence for convicted felons.

The best political reporters stayed on the beat their entire career. It took that long to learn it. One of the old-timers, who had covered politics for twenty-two years by the time I arrived, would often walk into the pressroom and ask, "How many times do you think we'll be lied to today?" He insisted it went with the territory. The trick was to be skeptical without becoming cynical. Our job, he said, was to report what newsmakers *said*, what they *meant* and what was *true*—regardless of whether the three matched. They often didn't.

As a public relations consultant, I work from the other side of the desk, helping companies shape their messages for media consumption. I help make sure the messages reflect what they mean and what is true. It's a critical exercise if a company wants to be "heard" and believed in this age of unprecedented information clutter.

I help clients wrestle with several basic questions:

- *Who are you talking to?* It's not uncommon for a company to be so self-absorbed with what they have to say that they ignore who they're saying it *to* or whether their audience is ready to hear them.

- *What's your objective?* What's the goal? What outcome are you looking for?

- *What's your key message?* Pretend you have thirty seconds to tell a sixteen-year-old the most important thing you want him to know about you, in language he will understand. Strip away all the window dressing. What's the most important thing you want to say?

- *Why should anyone believe you?* What objective information can you produce to support your message? Facts? Statistics? Anecdotes? The endorsement of your message by third parties?

Answering these questions keeps a company's words on target. It surfaces true motives and intentions and exposes inconsistencies. If a company faithfully works the process, they will arrive at words that powerfully communicate who they are and what they stand for.

I believe our personal words can benefit from the same scrutiny. We're less likely to run amok—especially when strong emotions are involved—if our own speech passes through the same grid of questions.

Who am I talking to, and are they ready to hear me? What, truthfully, do I hope to accomplish with these words? When I strip away the excessive explanations, excuses and efforts to control or impress, what am I trying to say? Can I skip the unnecessaries and get to the point? Is there objective information I can add to underscore the validity of my message?

It sounds impossible at first blush. Who's got the time and patience to go through all that every time we open our mouth? The monthly management report is due at the copy center in twenty minutes, and the computers just went down. My three-year-old just put lipstick on the dog, and the dog wiped it off on the carpet. A client snapped at me, and I want to snap back. There's a crisis. There's pressure. As one person said, "Mistakes have been made! Others must be blamed!" And I'm supposed to pause and evaluate my words? Get real!

You're right. The time for assessment is not in the heat of the moment or after words have left our lips. At that point their only value is to serve as a barometer of the condition of our heart. It's our job at that point—like a political beat reporter—to figure out if what we *said* is what we *meant* to say and if it's *true*. If there's no alignment, the only power our words carry is the power to maim. Then it's time to get alone with God and do the work on our words we should have done in the first place.

James 3:5 compares the tongue to a spark capable of setting an entire forest ablaze. Why, then, would we give our speech less thought than we use to order pizza?

The Psalms and Proverbs are a good place to start reevaluating our speech. If you want to know what God thinks about slander, gossip, lying, boasting, nagging, blaming, criticism, swearing, coarse joking and more . . . it's in there. There's instruction about how to speak, what to say, when to say it and when not to bother trying.

Here are a few general instructions to start:

- *It takes a personal commitment to change.* "I have resolved that my mouth will not sin." (Psalm 17:3)

- *We can't solve this problem by sheer willpower.* "Set a guard over my mouth, O LORD; keep watch over the door of my lips." (141:3)

- *If we're smart, we'll rein in our words and proceed with caution.* "A man of knowledge uses words with restraint." (Proverbs 17:27)

- *God has a standard of behavior for our words, regardless of what we may think is OK.* "Do not let any unwholesome talk come out of your mouths, but only what is helpful for building others up according to their needs, that it may benefit those who listen." (Ephesians 4:29)

Think about it as if you and God were creating a personal communication strategic plan. You've tackled bigger challenges than this. You can do it. God is in your corner on this one. In the end, your words will communicate with greater power. People will listen. And what you *say*, what you *meant* and what is *true* will live together in perfect harmony.

Reality

☐ Do your words get you in trouble?

☐ What area of speech poses the greatest challenge?

☐ What stop-actions can you take in the future to cut off this pattern of speech before the words leave your lips?

☐ Think of a recent situation where you felt you failed to speak appropriately. What would have been another way of handling it? Take a practice run at saying now what you wish you had said then.

Hostage to My Hurts

On March 22, 1997, Chicago newspaper headlines blurted out the awful story of what happened to Lenard Clark. The thirteen-year-old African-America boy was beaten into a coma by a group of white youths in the working-class neighborhood where Chicago's mayor lived. The savage beating triggered national media attention, local marches and a denunciation from the President.

While I shared the public's outrage, I wasn't surprised. As a reporter, I've covered too many stories that redefined evil. I've reported on drugged-out parents who placed their baby in a bathtub and electrocuted him for crying too much. I've reported on a young man who ran over a little old lady with his sport utility vehicle because she took too long to cross the street.

I have trouble believing that anyone who has a pulse and reads a newspaper can still believe that man at his core is basically good. The daily news is the best example I can offer of the need for redemption of the human heart.

Lenard Clark's chief attacker, nineteen-year-old Frank Caruso, Jr., was eventually sentenced to eight years in prison for the beating. The public expressed collective relief that punishment had been exacted.

Some said it played out the immutable law of sowing and reaping. Job 4:8 says, "Those who plow evil and those who sow trouble reap it." Even people with no religious beliefs understood instinctively that actions ought to have consequences. Somebody must pay.

What didn't make sense to many people was what happened two years after the beating. Lenard Clark began to meet with his attacker to extend forgiveness. When their private meetings came to light, skeptics went ballistic. Clark was breaking the rules. To forgive was tantamount to condoning the violence, they implied. "Lenard Clark was probably coerced into meeting with Caruso," some said. "It's a hoax. It's a stunt. It's a ploy to get the assailant's jail term reduced." The question behind the questions was, "What was Clark thinking? Forgiveness? Is he nuts?"

One of the main ironies of forgiveness is that we don't forgive someone for the other person's sake. We forgive for *our* sake—to release the hold the person's sin has had on *our* heart so we can get on with life. Forgiveness doesn't excuse the offense or minimize it. It doesn't mean we forget what happened. It means we are no longer held captive by the wrong done against us. It can't yank our chain anymore.

It isn't as easy as it sounds on paper. We know intellectually that God commanded us to forgive as an act of obedience. "Forgive, and you will be forgiven" (Luke 6:37). But finding the "want to" is another story.

Besides, we may tell ourselves, if a wrong against us is not of the magnitude of Lenard Clark's beating, it probably doesn't require formal forgiveness. Let's not make a big deal out of it, OK?

The real question is whether the incident is truly not a big deal or whether we've dismissed it because we're not ready to forgive.

Forgive? Did you forget what they did to me? *Somebody must pay.*

Let's say your boss gives you a mediocre performance review because you're too good, and he fears you might be his replacement. Or maybe your child fails to win a spot on the neighborhood softball team because he plays the same position as the coach's son—and plays it better. Are you willing to forgive and let go of your anger and judgments? Or do you prefer to carry the wrongs around in your pocket for awhile, report them to as many people as possible and think about ways to return the favor?

When a friend or spouse suggests forgiveness, you say, "Hey, they're jerks. I'm not wasting another minute of my time thinking about them." But if a gnawing irritation, resentment or bitterness bubbles just below the radar, they have not been, in fact, dismissed. There's unfinished business—forgiveness business—for your sake as well as theirs.

God did not say forgiveness was contingent on a hierarchy of wrongs. He didn't say, "If you spent time in a concentration camp or if your child was killed by a hit-and-run driver, you can forget the forgiveness thing." The command was simply to forgive—always—because none of us had to pay God for our sins.

Psalm 103:10 says, "He does not treat us as our sins deserve." Our own sin debt should have earned us a life sentence from God, so where do we get off withholding forgiveness from someone else? The only difference between a mass murderer and me is that my sins haven't made the front page of the *Chicago Tribune*.

Ranking our sins against others or the sins committed against us doesn't work. God doesn't grade on a curve. Besides, the net effect is the same for all of us. It cuts us off from God and carries a price tag we can't possibly pay—which circles us back to the command to forgive. We're to just *do* it and quit the tap dancing.

I met two people in Johannesburg, South Africa, who were a living testimony to irrational forgiveness. I met them at a church conference held shortly after apartheid officially ended. It was the first time blacks had worshiped together with whites in that church. It was full of awkward moments. No one knew how to act. The years of hatred did not magically fall away.

During a tea break, I met Ethel and Ferguson, cousins who must have been in their eighties. They had traveled fourteen hours from Transkie, one of the black homelands, to attend the conference.

Ferguson had powerful spiritual gifts of pastoring and evangelism. For years, though, a group of people who wanted to discredit him and discredit what God was doing in his life had accused him of being a witch doctor. It broke his heart, because it meant some people wouldn't listen to the good news of the gospel he wanted to share.

His shoulders sloped and his face bore a certain life-weariness, but he never mentioned the slander. I learned his story from someone else. What was unmistakable was the sweetness of his spirit. You could almost taste it. The emotional pain was evident, but there was not a trace of bitterness. Unforgiveness took too much precious time and energy. He stepped off that train a long time ago.

Ferguson understood that *somebody already paid*—Jesus, by His death on the cross. So every morning, you and I and Ferguson and Ethel *and* their accusers, *and* Lenard Clark *and* Frank Caruso, Jr., can face God with a clean record. No words can describe my relief and gratitude.

When you can't muster forgiveness out of pure obedience, do it instead as a living thank-you note. "I'll forgive this person because of You, Jesus. Thanks for picking up my tab."

Reality

☐ What people or events in your life continue to cause pain because they represent unfinished business?

☐ What have you been hoping would happen before you're willing to forgive?

☐ Is it a realistic expectation?

☐ Are you ready to talk to God about where you're stuck and give Him permission to change your heart?

Is It Safe to Open My Eyes Yet?

There is nothing compelling about socks. Who thinks about them unless your company makes socks that keep feet warm in subzero weather and you can't get the buying public to sit up and take notice? Let's face it, it would take more than a nifty advertising campaign and a mention in *Sox Journal* to position you as *the* leader in socks. It's the kind of challenge marketing professionals fret over every day.

Whatever strategy is ultimately employed, the key is to make it simple and attention-grabbing. We call it "dumbing it down." For example (work with me on this), we could create a national Feet Feats Day and get famous people to perform acts of daring in frigid temperatures— wearing only socks. Or what about a Cold Feet Survey to identify who has the coldest feet—men or women? There would be a few serious questions on the survey, of course, but it could be fun and educational. How often can you say that about socks?

Assuming the survey was conducted by a reputable market research firm and the results held at least modest news value, media outlets might give it feature coverage—especially on a slow news day. And our pretend sock manufacturer who commissioned the survey would receive free publicity, generate customer goodwill and build brand recognition as a leader in his industry.

I'm a consultant. I don't sell socks. I sell my expertise in areas like media training, public relations strategic planning, business writing and related services. The sock example got me thinking about the things I know how to do which, heretofore, I haven't capitalized on. Hands down, it is my ability to worry.

I worry equally well in all time zones. I worry about things that haven't happened yet. And I'm especially good at worrying over both my problems and other people's. Is this a great gift or what?

Maybe I should host a National Worry Symposium. The theme could be, "Worry for a New Millennium: Have You Been There and Done That? Come and Learn How to Do It Some More." Don't tell me only women need this kind of event. Four out of five men worry. I took a poll.

I'd arrange workshops like, "Eradicating Happiness in Our Lifetime," "Ten Surefire Ways to Maximize Your Misery" and "Power Pity: The Secret to Worry That Lasts."

I wish I could dismiss my tendency to worry as a laughable but benign habit. Unfortunately, Jesus was pretty blunt about worrying—don't do it! It's not advice I can pretend I don't understand.

It's spelled out in Luke 12 (repeated in Matthew 6) where a crowd had gathered to listen as Jesus explained to the disciples the perks and demands of their new life as His right-hand men.

They had left everything to follow Jesus. They had no 401-K to fall back on. When their sandals wore out, they couldn't pop into the nearest J.C. Penney's and charge new shoes on their Visa card. They put it all on the line.

It was in that context that Jesus said,

> Don't worry about life, wondering what you are going to eat, or what clothes your body will need. Life is much more important than food, and the body more important than clothes. Think of the ravens. They neither sow nor reap, and they have neither store nor barn, but God feeds them. And how much more valuable do you think you are than birds? Can any of you make himself even a few inches taller however much he worries about it? And if you can't manage a little thing like this, why do you worry about anything else? (Luke 12:22-26, Phillips)

Jesus makes clear that worrying is an invitation to irresponsible behavior. The disciples had a job to do. Refraining from worry was about getting their priorities straight—investing time and energy in the right places and not spending time on things they couldn't do anything about, like making themselves taller! The benefits of worrying, Jesus says, are zip, zero, nada.

A few verses later He adds, "O you of little faith" (12:28). I picture Jesus breathing a deep sigh, as if to say, "You still don't get it, do you? It's the trust thing. You don't do it once at the beginning. You have to trust Me everyday."

Jesus wasn't offering His counsel as an off-the-cuff suggestion, like, "Oh, by the way guys, if you ever feel tense, you might want to try this little biofeedback exercise." He was telling them what it would take to survive a new life that did not include their usual safety net of family, friends and traditional income.

It was as if He was saying, "Fellows, it's not up to you anymore. When you didn't know your heavenly Father, you had reason to worry . . . but you're His kids now, remember? Your needs are God's responsibility. Take care of His business, and He'll take care of yours."

When I admit the ways I camouflage excessive planning and control and worry by calling it "prudence" and "concern," it looks painfully like someone who's not sure God will deliver what I need when I need it. I fail to factor in God.

We aren't hanging out there on our own anymore. Our heavenly Father knows that the kids need braces and the real estate taxes are due next month. "But seek first his kingdom and his righteousness, and all these things will be given to you as well" (Matthew 6:33). Work hard, manage your time and resources responsibly, but keep your priorities straight. If you must worry, then worry over the things that break the heart of God—like the poor, the hurting and the spiritually lost people you know.

It's a challenge. I think trusting God is harder than running a business. I'll try not to worry about it.

☐ What has inappropriately troubled you today?

☐ Can you do anything about it?

☐ What is your part?

☐ What is God's part?

☐ Do you believe He'll give you what you need when you need it?

☐ Do you have a clear understanding of the difference between appropriate concern and worry?

☐ Do your priorities need to be rearranged?

PART TWO:

Taming Our Outer World

The Battle for Margin

What thoughts come to mind when people suggest you slow down and exercise a little moderation in your life, especially in your career? Do you feel stifled? Does it sound dull? Do you think they should get lives of their own to run? We live in a culture where balance is defined as the ability to juggle too many things without the sky falling in on us.

I was traveling on the expressway yesterday in heavy traffic. Everyone was pushing the speed limit in unison. In an instant, the driver in the car beside me began to swerve wildly, almost losing control before steadying his car. When I looked over at him, he was eating a sandwich in one hand, writing on a notepad on the dashboard with the other hand, steering with his elbows and wearing a headset while talking on his cell phone. (I'm not making this up.) What a pity he couldn't find something for his toes to do!

I hate the unspoken pressure that says to live at any pace less than full tilt is tantamount to being a slacker. In a cover story entitled, "Finished at Forty," *Fortune* magazine reported on the increasing number of corporations that are discarding middle management executives before they hit midlife because they've stopped running hard enough. The article suggests that by the time these executives reach their forties—working sixty- to eighty-hour weeks for years—they wake up to the personal costs and want more time for family, church, leisure and community involvement. If they pull back even slightly, the corporate response is to cast them aside for twenty-somethings still willing to sacrifice everything to be "in the game."[1]

The tactics send a strong message: "These are the rules. Play by them or get hurt." Anyone who chooses to stop living in crisis mode is an anomaly. It's not the way the world works anymore.

One way Jesus maintained His equilibrium during His three years of active ministry was to withdraw to "lonely places" and pray. He got away from the push-push-shove-shove around Him to talk to God about His marching orders. (" . . . I do nothing on my own but speak just what the Father has taught me. The one who sent me is with me; he has not left me alone, for I always do what pleases him" [John 8:28-29].) He let His Father shape His values, change His priorities, lay out His next steps and prepare His heart to carry them out.

In Ephesians chapter 5, we're encouraged to follow the same model—to be "imitators of God" (5:1), to "find out what pleases the Lord" (5:10) and to value the things He holds dear (5:3-5, 9, 11, 18-20). Once we get alone with God to reassess the pace and content of our lives, a few things become apparent.

First, it requires resolve to change the way things are. C.S. Lewis said,

> Progress means getting nearer to the place where you want to be. If you have taken a wrong turn, then to go forward does not get you any nearer. If you are on the wrong road, progress means doing an about-turn and walking back to the right road.[2]

No one, with the possible exception of a spouse or your mother, is interested in whether you have a balanced life. You yourself have to make it a core value of your life and fight for it on a daily basis. The fight will be useless unless God coaches you and you allow Christian brothers and sisters to cheer you on and remind you of your commitment. We can't do it alone.

Second, it requires action, not just a change of attitude. God is on your side in this battle for balance. The life you were meant to live was not meant to include unrelenting physical exhaustion, emotional disillusionment, a shriveled heart, damaged relationships, spiritual dryness and all the other consequences of living life with no margin. Here's the catch. He needs your undivided attention to guide you back to sanity, and He needs your willingness to act on what He leads you to do. All of it.

Third, it will rock the boat. When you stop playing by the rules of this world, the world pushes back. Count on it. It may be a rough transition that will test how serious you are about this. First Peter 4:12 warns, "Do not be surprised at the painful trial you are suffering, as though something strange were happening to you." It will cost something. Why should that surprise us? Everything has a price. The cost of an *un*balanced life is no bargain.

God's remedy may also rock the boat of your own expectations. He may ask you to pare down the number of activities you are involved in—all of which are good and all of which you love—or pass up a promotion that carries with it unreasonable demands on your time. He may ask you to rein in your wants so that financial debt is not driving your decisions.

Jeremiah 6:16 urges, "Stand at the crossroads and look . . . ask where the good way is, and walk in it, and you will find rest for your souls."

What is the payoff for balance? Rest. Finally.

Reality

- ☐ What areas of your life are most out of balance right now?

- ☐ What consequences are you feeling physically, mentally, spiritually and emotionally?

- ☐ Are you ready to listen to God about this?

- ☐ Ask Him what is one thing you can do immediately to move in the direction of balance. Write it down here and date it as a reminder of the commitment you're making. Give yourself a deadline by which you will revisit this issue and explore it in more detail.

  - I commit to _____ as a first step to a more balanced life.

  - By _____ (date) I will have taken a closer look at this and asked God to help me craft a specific action plan for a lifestyle that better reflects His values.

    Date _____

Yours, Mine and You-Know-Whose

I used to collect barbed wire. I know. It's weird. It started years ago when I found some odd-looking barbed wire on undeveloped land purchased by my dad. I was curious why someone would go to the trouble of designing his very own style "barb" and why there needed to be barbs at all. I was, after all, basically a city girl, and the wire looked rather, well, barbaric. (Sorry, I couldn't help myself.)

Upon further investigation, I learned that there are nearly 600 kinds of barbed wire—each carefully catalogued in a book titled, ironically, The "Bobbed Wire" Bible. (Who else tells you these things?)

I collected more than 100 different kinds of barbed wire before I tired of the hobby. (Actually, what I tired of was the strange looks I got for trying to decorate a family room around a wall of eighteen-inch strips of wire designed to inflict pain.)

Barbed wire has an interesting history. It was created to keep livestock *in* rather than to keep people or animals *out*, which had been the purpose of fencing to that point. In New England, early settlers used rocks to build wall-like fences. It kept wild critters from eating their gardens. In the mid-Atlantic and southern states, fences were made of wood, taken from lush forests nearby.

When settlers moved west to the plains states, the land was not rocky or forested, so, at first, they strung wire between wood posts. But livestock raised in pole corrals walked through plain wiring fencing as though it didn't exist. Adding pointed barbs helped solve the problem. The barb sent a painful message to reinforce what was to be their turf and what was someone else's turf. It clarified boundaries.

God sets boundaries in our relationship with Him as well, although we're not all on the same page about what those boundaries are. Among the more amusing misconceptions is that "God helps those who help themselves" is one of God's rules and one of the Ten Commandments. Ben Franklin would be offended.

True, the Ten Commandments and other clear directives in Scripture teach us what is appropriate behavior. But God also sets boundaries for what belongs to Him and what is ours.

If you want to know how God draws property lines, it works like this. God's part: 100 percent. Our part: 0 percent. It's not something most of us accept without debate. We're prone to negotiating with God about the percentages.

On one occasion in Scripture, James and John, the sons of Zebedee, approached Jesus and tried to cash in on their close relationship. " 'Teacher,' they said, 'we want you to do for us whatever we ask' " (Mark 10:35). They asked Jesus to assure them positions of prestige and power—the seats at His right and left hands—when He was finally recognized as Messiah. They thought they had a bargaining chip as members of Jesus' inner circle.

Fuhgedaboutit!

Jesus pointedly replied, "You don't know what you're asking" (10:38). They clearly didn't understand what was theirs and what wasn't. Jesus told them that the spots on either side of Him were not His to grant.

When the rich young ruler in Luke 18 asked Jesus what it took to inherit eternal life, the man pointed out that he had kept all the commandments since he was a boy. That ought to count for something, right? Jesus told him, "You still lack one thing. Sell everything you have and give to the poor, and you will have treasure in heaven. *Then* come, follow me" (18:22, emphasis added).

We don't get to use our titles, wealth, looks, fame or even our spiritual zeal or service to improve our standing in God's pecking order. We're custodians, not owners.

Jesus wasn't trying to be nasty about it. He just basically said, "You asked. Here's what it takes. You no longer get to define yourself by your 'stuff.' "

The Bible says the rich young ruler went away sad because he was a man of great wealth. "Jesus looked at him and said, 'How hard it is for the rich to enter the kingdom of God!' " (18:24).

Jesus wasn't saying it was too bad the man was wealthy. The Bible is full of people like Joseph, David, Esther and Daniel who went from obscurity to prominence and reached the pinnacles of power—with God's blessing. Many of them enjoyed great wealth and abundant possessions. The ones who got into trouble were the ones who forgot it wasn't their stuff.

Jesus was stating the obvious. It's hard for people who bring a lot to the party to lay down identifying themselves by their assets and résumés. People of modest means already know their poverty.

I think the rich young ruler went away sad because he wanted to continue to be identified as a righteous-but-nevertheless-still-rich young ruler. He couldn't hold loosely his assets and the trappings that accompanied them. He wanted them to stay on *his* side of the fence. He forgot they weren't his in the first place.

John Ortberg tells the story of his competitiveness as a child playing Monopoly with the passion of a mogul. Aggressively he would snatch up Park Place, Boardwalk and all the other expensive properties on the board game until he had amassed a paper fortune.

When he began to gloat about all he owned and how he had outdistanced his closest rivals, his grandmother would gently remind him, "Johnny, just remember, when the game is over, it all goes back in the box."

Reality

☐ Could you lose your strongest assets tomorrow—financial or otherwise—and still feel OK about yourself?

☐ What are the things in your life that are easy to let go of, and which things do you still cling to like an owner rather than a custodian?

☐ What do you like about God's level playing field?

☐ What bothers you?

☐ Talk to God about what's hard.

When My "Get-up-and-Go" . . . Won't

A television documentary not long ago described workaholism as America's best-dressed addiction and one of our country's most unheralded family crises.

The report focused not only on the pace of modern life (which I talk about in the chapter on balance) or how much we try to cram in each day (discussed in the chapter on limitations), but also described how people don't know how to stop until it's too late. It's as if someone turned off the light at the end of the tunnel. We keep careening forward at breakneck speed until we crash and burn.

I vividly recall when I flamed out. I worked as a middle manager for a regional health care conglomerate. It was challenging work with colleagues I respected. Prospects for the future—mine and theirs—were rosy.

Then health care reform dropped into the mix, and the industry began to consolidate rapidly as a hedge against managed care. Our company entered into merger talks with another major health care conglomerate to assure continued dominance in the field.

Executives from both organizations began to jump ship, knowing the merger would eliminate many of their positions. My boss left, taking two managers with her. I was offered a shot at her job but declined. It was not a good fit for my gifts and long-term goals. I agreed to serve as Acting Director in the interim and was told recruiters would begin an immediate search for replacements—a statement that, in retrospect, ranks right up there with "the check is in the mail."

Over the next several weeks, other staffers left. The workload increased, and the hours got longer and longer. We hunkered down, telling ourselves, "It's temporary. We can take it. Besides, we're helping to write the book on the brave new world of health care."

Three months later, not a single candidate had come through the department for any of the open positions. When I began to press for an explanation, I was told that everything was on hold until after the merger—which was still months away. I was too busy trying to survive the next deadline to step back and see the inevitability of what happened next.

One night, I left the office quite late after another marathon day. I got into my car and reached out to put the key in the ignition. My arm fell limp to my side like a rag doll's.

I couldn't lift it. To make matters worse, I was so mentally fatigued I struggled to formulate other options to get myself home. It was like everything died at once.

As I sat in the parking lot—of a hospital, no less!—staring at the red neon light 100 yards away that said "Emergency," I thought, *You are in serious trouble, lady. And it will take more than a good night's rest to fix it.*

If this were a public relations crisis for a corporate client, I would have urged them to assemble a crisis team of trusted senior advisors to act swiftly and decisively to create an action plan. I would encourage them to identify a chief spokesperson, move quickly to protect the injured parties, launch an investigation into the cause and do whatever it takes to assure it will never happen again.

When a Christian faces a personal burnout crisis, many of the same principles apply—except God is at the table and at the center of all plans (immediate and long-term) and, hands down, ought to be our designated chief spokesperson.

Why God? What has He got to do with this kind of crisis? Well, He is the original manufacturer of us and our lives. Burnout indicates that we, the end user, are not properly using what He created. He needs to retool and recalibrate us and review the operating instructions with us again. There was nothing wrong with what He made when it left the factory. It's what we've done with it since.

"If any of you lacks wisdom, he should ask God, who gives generously to all without finding fault, and it will be given to him" (James 1:5). If anyone knows the best way out of your mess, it's God.

Nothing will happen if we are personally in burnout mode until we acknowledge there is a problem. Then, if we want a different outcome, we must make different choices. One of our most important decisions will be to get help.

How does God deliver His rescue plan? It will come through Scripture, circumstances, the Holy Spirit's promptings as we pray and the wise counsel of mature Christians friends who come alongside us in the crisis and have our best interests at heart. Christian professional help may be appropriate too. Like it or not, God made us dependent creatures. This is not something we can fix alone.

When help comes—just as if it were a corporate crisis—we must be willing to do whatever it takes to make sure it doesn't happen again. And we can thank God He stepped in before it was too late.

In Old Testament times, terrifying storms often arose in the Mediterranean Sea. When God would calm the seas, the Israelites were filled with great relief and praise. Psalm 107:26-31 was written to thank God for hearing and answering the prayers of those caught at sea during such storms. They sang it every year at one of their festivals.

> In their peril their courage melted away.
> They reeled and staggered like drunken men;
> they were at their wits' end.
> Then they cried out to the LORD in their
> trouble,
> and he brought them out of their distress.
> He stilled the storm to a whisper;
> the waves of the sea were hushed.

They were glad when it grew calm,
> and he guided them to their desired haven.
Let them give thanks to the LORD for his
> unfailing love
> and his wonderful deeds for men.

(107:26-31)

Storms come. Sometimes we're victims of them, and sometimes we cause them. Either way, we need to find a safe harbor. God knows how to get there.

Reality

- ☐ How well are you managing the pace of your life?

- ☐ Do you see any warning signs of burnout?

- ☐ Do you have a few trusted close friends or family members who can give you an honest appraisal of how you are doing in this area?

- ☐ Has God been giving you early-warning signals through circumstances or a sense in your spirit that something is out of kilter?

- ☐ Act decisively on what you know in order to avert more drastic consequences.

Disturbing the Peace and Other Crimes

For 350 years the kingdom of Bhutan existed in self-imposed isolation in a pocket of the Eastern Himalayas between India and China. The country had no roads, no currency, no crime, no electricity and no TV. By all accounts, no one went hungry. The people lived in peace with their neighbors. They got along fine without the things most of us think we need for a good life.

Explorers who visited the region called it "The Last Shangri-La." As word spread about this tiny remote country untouched by change, people wanted to go there.

A few years ago, the king relented, decreeing that 5,000 tourists a year would be allowed to visit the hidden kingdom. Recently, television also came to Bhutan. Although the king limited programming to two hours a day, hoping to keep out harmful western influences, the cat was out of the bag. Tourism and television signaled the end of innocence for Bhutan.

Most of us look wistfully at a place like Bhutan as a safe haven from a world that's careening into the future at the speed of light. The pace and level of change in our culture is unnerving. The entire store of human knowledge now doubles every five years. There is more to keep track of than ever before and fewer things about which we can be certain. If only we could find another Bhutan where time stands still, where we could wrap our arms around the good stuff before it gets away.

Frankly, I suspect God is glad we're running out of Bhutans. It forces us to confront the hapless notion that (a) change is a bad thing to be tightly controlled and its companion corollary; (b) happiness is dependent on locking into place the right circumstances.

Change, after all, is what God is all about. From one end of the Bible to the other, He is on the move, stirring things up. As C.S. Lewis once said, God just won't settle down.

In Isaiah 43:18-19, God told the children of Israel, "Forget the former things; do not dwell on the past. See, I am doing a new thing!" God is always doing a new thing, whether He's playing the involved parent, intensely interested in what happens to His children, or superintending the affairs of mankind as sovereign of all creation. He's not only alive and well. He's busy.

When I read Scripture, I try to imagine what it felt like to be Moses or Joseph or Daniel or Esther or Elizabeth or blind Bartimaeus or others whose lives God or Jesus interrupted. Sometimes I picture myself with Jesus when He walked the earth. He's out in front of me going full tilt, and I'm breathlessly running along behind, hurling questions like, "Where are we going, Jesus? Why did You just do *that*?" But I can't get Him to turn around and explain!

God is not insensitive to our anxieties. In Isaiah 43:1-5, He poured out words of encouragement to the children of Israel, even as He alerted them to the tough times ahead:

- "I have summoned you by name."

- "When you pass through the waters, . . . they will not sweep over you."

- "When you will walk through the fire, you will not be burned."

- "You are precious and honored in my sight."

- "I love you."

- "I will give men in exchange for you."

- "Do not be afraid, for I am with you."

"Relax," God said. "Change is tough, but you're not hanging out there on your own. We'll get through this."

One of the most poignant metaphors in Scripture is found in Isaiah 49:15: "Can a mother forget the baby at her breast and have no compassion on the child she has borne? Though she may forget, I will not forget you!" God says a nursing mother is more likely to abandon her child than the Lord is likely to abandon us. Any mother who has nursed an infant understands the absurdity of such a thought. He's a hands-on heavenly Father, utterly concerned with the welfare of His children.

If you feel like the country of Bhutan—fighting to keep change at bay—you're wasting your time. If you must fear something, fear tiny plans and rigid thinking. Fear getting in the way of God's plan for you. Because change is God's 24-7 job.

Reality

☐ What changes in your past have been painful?

☐ Have you worked through those experiences with God and let them go?

☐ What is it about change that is most distressing?

☐ Do you live life like a person who believes God is constantly at your side?

☐ Discuss with God any fears you have about trusting Him for changes that are coming in the future.

☐ As you are reading Scripture, each time you come across a promise of God's commitment to you, list the reference on a page in the back of your Bible. Refer to those verses when you're going through a difficult transition.

"Kumbaya" Won't Help Us Now

f you read the list of Nobel Peace Prize honorees and why they are honored, you get a blunt reminder how hard it is for human beings to get along. We bestow the highest peace honor in the world on those in tough places like Northern Ireland, the Middle East, East Timor, South Africa and Central America who devote their lives to convincing people to live in harmony. The fact that these regions continue to be hotbeds of conflict shows how tough a job it is.

Sometimes, when I read a story about man's inhumanity to man, I think, smugly, *Don't these people have better things to do than kill each other? Can't they sit down around the table and work this out?* It seems like there ought to be a way.

Then a neighbor's dog destroys my perennial flowerbed because the neighbor thinks the local leash laws are for everyone's dog but his. A teenage hothead cuts me off on the expressway and gives me a hand sign that definitely does not symbolize peace. An insufferable colleague "powers up" on me in a client meeting. A vendor blows off a production deadline, leaving me to deal with outraged customers. And it's only 11 a.m.!

My peace-and-love flower-child talk goes right out the window. I want to push back. All that "turn-the-other-cheek" business suddenly seems like a pathetic way to deal with an adversary who thinks I would look pretty good cut off at the knees.

What's the deal, God? I think. *Surely You don't expect me to stand by and let them get away with this?*

And therein lies the heart of the matter. Resolution is defined as getting everybody onto *my page*. Isn't that the way we frame most conflicts? Who gets to have his way? Who wins?

I recently interviewed a woman who runs one of the largest social service agencies in the Chicago area that serves abused and battered women. She said the number of women they serve has increased 250 percent in just two years, a startling statistic considering the economic good times. While I shuddered at what it must take to cope with such explosive need, she wanted to talk about the other startling thing that was happening, which she found even more amazing—a collaborative spirit that was emerging among those addressing the problem.

For twenty years, she said, the police departments, the courts, medical professionals, municipal officials and social service providers all engaged in turf battles, in-fighting and misunderstanding—a scenario common to almost every arena of life. When the problem of domestic violence got so overwhelming they couldn't afford the luxury of such conflict, it forced them to start focusing on solutions instead of blame. Now they're working together to meet the urgent need.

"They used to refer to us as 'those women,'" the woman said. "Today the system is working. I didn't think I'd live long enough to see this happen. It's wonderful."

I asked her what turned things around. She pointed to several valuable lessons they had learned about resolving disagreements:

- Realize there's another point of view.

- Listen as much as you talk.

- Own the ways in which you are contributing to the problem.

I added her counsel to other advice I've heard over the years from friends, pastors, therapists and professional negotiators.

- Ask yourself, *Whose problem is this?*

- Identify your unspoken expectations. Are you more interested in being right than preserving the relationship?

- Listen one minute longer than necessary.

- Detach. Take a "time-out" to cool off before responding.

As Christians, we have the double benefit of Scripture's counsel for how to handle our intramural conflicts. Colossians 3:13-14 says, "Put up with each other, and forgive anyone who does you wrong, just as Christ has forgiven you. Love is more important than anything else. It is what ties everything completely together" (CEV). Matthew 18 spells out how to handle the conflicts that get extra messy.

Unity is championed so strongly throughout the Bible that I keep expecting a cheerleader to leap out of some chapter and yell, "Give me a U, give me an N, give me an I. . . ."

With all that help and encouragement inside and outside of Scripture, why can't we just do it? Because ultimately it's not a matter of more information—it's a matter of the condition of our heart.

Any conflict will be handled as maturely as the less mature and less emotionally healthy person in the relationship. In the end, the most valuable thing that may happen in a conflict is not that we win but what it can teach us about ourselves and where we need to grow.

I have no intention of stepping out into a rugged world and hanging a doormat around my neck that says, "Please Step Here." But it's also naive to think that another how-to course in conflict resolution is all I need in order to make everyone behave.

Every day I must bring my strong will and banged-up heart to God for reshaping and renewal. Otherwise, I'll be just another casualty of war or responsible for an embarrassing number of "kills" of my own.

Reality

- [ ] What has been the typical way I handle conflict?

- [ ] Do I handle problems differently with Christians and non-Christians? Should I?

- [ ] What is my biggest struggle when I'm in a tense situation with another person?

- [ ] What would be helpful for me to work through now, knowing this kind of situation will probably come up again?

Making Life Behave

The Associated Press wire service reported a story about a Pennsylvania man who filed a lawsuit against God for not bringing him justice in a thirty-year battle against his former employer, U.S. Steel (now USX Corporation). In his complaint, plaintiff Donald Drusky also asked God to restore his youth, resurrect his mother and grant him the musical skills of famous guitarists. Drusky argued that if God failed to appear in court to answer the charges, federal rules of civil procedure dictated that God, by default, would lose. A federal judge dismissed the suit.

This is known as a "kicker" story in the news business—an offbeat or amusing story designed to elicit a grin or incredulous shake of the head.

Although the lawsuit was patently frivolous, most of us can identify with Drusky's desire for more control over life. We work hard to assure a secure future. We accumulate money as a hedge against changing circumstances. As we age, we gain more power and authority so we can minimize what others can do to us. And when our best efforts at control fail, privately we say, "God, You've got some explaining to do."

"What about that drunk driver that careened into my car and left me with months of physical pain. What was *that* all about?" Or maybe it was the malignant tumor despite no family history of cancer. Or a close friend's business failure after twenty-five successful years. Or the spouse who decided he couldn't do the marriage thing anymore.

"I need to know," we tell God. Implied in the statement is, "You owe me an explanation." The truth is, it's seldom about knowing. What we really want is control—a way to feel safe in an uncertain world. It's ludicrous, though. We can't nail down *all* the variables. We're setting ourselves up for repeated disappointment to believe otherwise.

My own Achilles' heel is computers. I have enough computer stories to entertain a convention of geeks for a week. They aren't even glamorous stories of harrowing near misses from some mutant virus.

They are stories like what happened shortly after I went out on my own as a consultant. I was working from my home office and up against an impossible deadline with a potential new client. I was a late entry to their consultant selection process. They said if I faxed my proposal to them by 4 o'clock I would be among the entries considered when their management committee discussed the proposals at a dinner meeting that evening.

I worked like a madwoman putting the finishing touches on a thirty-page proposal when, without warning, the screen went black, and all the electricity in my house went out. I sat in twilight in total shock. Outside, tradesmen were screaming at each other and a man sitting atop a piece of earth-moving equipment was shouting into his cell phone. In the process of excavating for a new home to be built nearby, he had accidentally severed the main electric utility line, knocking out power to the whole area. The transformer was damaged. It would be the next day before power was restored.

The proposal was sealed away in the memory of my dead computer hard drive. There was not a thing I could do. I had the latest equipment, the latest software, a complete back-up system; everything was under control. Yet a guy pushing dirt around stopped me dead in my tracks.

The hard reality is that control can't deliver what it promises. It can't guarantee the absence of pain or restore what's lost. And it will never be enough to make us feel safe because tomorrow a fresh set of circumstances will change the picture yet again.

The Bible calls King Solomon the wisest man who ever lived. First Kings 4 says Solomon wrote 3,000 wise sayings and 1,000 songs. What's more, he had an international reputation for his knowledge of the natural world. People came from all over the known world to learn from him. His understanding of life was said to be "as measureless as the sand on the seashore" (I Kings

4:29). But even Solomon knew you couldn't make life behave.

In words attributed to him in Ecclesiastes 8:17 he says, "No one can comprehend what goes on under the sun. Despite all his efforts to search it out, man cannot discover its meaning. Even if a wise man claims he knows, he cannot really comprehend it."

Stability doesn't come from having all the answers. It isn't a by-product of being in control. It comes from being anchored to something outside me that doesn't move. God says, in essence, "That would be Me, but answers aren't necessarily part of the package."

Giving up the need to control is a process, not an event. The more unpleasant the surprises we've experienced in life, the more we find that control is an issue. It is a survival tool of first resort. And when the need for it is diminished, it often takes up residence as an unhealthy habit.

The truth about control sticks to me lightly. Relinquishing control to God requires constant repetition until I form new habits. Thankfully, God is committed to me for the long haul. He's more invested in the person I am becoming than in whether I've arrived. I really wish He'd do something, though, about my computer.

Reality

☐ Is control a major issue in your life?

☐ Where does it hold the tightest grip?

☐ What is your earliest memory of being thrown into a tailspin by an unexpected event?

☐ How has that affected your attitude toward control?

☐ How much moving-around room are you willing to give God to disrupt your life if necessary?

☐ What are you willing to relinquish control over today?

The Devil Made Me Do It

Surfing on the internet, I ran across a web site that offers excuses for every occasion—work situations, skipping church, relationship problems, police trouble, diets, taxes and more. Whatever jam you could possibly find yourself in, they had it covered. Another company, for a fee, will create a credible alibi for you, including fake documentation for anything short of breaking the law.

Am I missing something here, or are we fostering a culture of tap dancers who've mastered the art of the sidestep? What ever happened to taking responsibility for our actions?

Excuses, when you strip away the smoke and mirrors, are frequently a way of avoiding consequences for actions that deserve consequences.

A computer hacker disabled the computer system of the Virginia Department of Motor Vehicles. He said the stupid policies of his car insurance company made him do it.

A mentally troubled felon killed an abortion clinic worker. He said the numbers on his social security card in his wallet "told" him to kill the woman. It was "their" fault.

In the country of Jordan, Human Rights Watch says thirty women a year are murdered by a family member who is either excused from punishment altogether or faces a reduced punishment. Why? The murders are considered "honor" killings. A perceived or alleged violation of the family's honor "excuses" the taking of a life. To add further insult, females who are at risk but have not yet been murdered are imprisoned . . . for their "protection." Huh? What's wrong with this picture?

If people can get away with murder by making excuses, no wonder we have trouble telling the difference between a legitimate explanation and a sidestepping excuse in our day-to-day lives where things are not nearly as black and white.

One of the quickest tests of whether an excuse is appropriate is to check our motives. Are we trying to get off the hook and justify unacceptable behavior? Or are we trying to truly clarify and inform, to avoid misunderstanding or an unfair judgment?

Here's an example. For years I struggled with being a performance-driven person. My excuse was that I was raised by a demanding father who dispensed and withheld love on the basis of how well I met his expectations, not on the basis of who I was. So I learned early on that the way to be loved and accepted was to perform. Lots of people can identify.

Later, as a manager, when I held the people who reported to me to a high standard, everyone understood why. I would say I wanted to push them to excellence. If I pushed too hard, I would trot out the story about my harsh upbringing by my father with its implied, "Excuse me for being a jerk." It covered all the bases.

Was it a helpful explanation or an excuse? It was a little of both. Eventually, I had to face the fact that my father was not a legitimate reason for riding people too hard. I needed to strike a balance between the push for excellence and the kind of pushing that said more about a flawed part of my character that the Holy Spirit wanted to tap for renovation.

I once knew an executive of a large company who shut the door to his Monday morning management meetings promptly at 7:30 a.m. If you arrived late by even five minutes and the door was shut, you were not permitted entrance. He didn't care if traffic was bad or if your alarm clock failed to go off because of a power outage or if your kid was up all night with the flu. He figured anybody smart enough to rise to a senior management position in the company ought to be able to figure out a way to plan for such contingencies and still get to the meeting on time.

While I believe his hard-and-fast rule was a bit over the top, it was amazing how punctuality improved when the fudge factor was removed and everyone knew their tardiness would draw nonnegotiable consequences. It was a crude but effective way of weeding out excuses that had no merit.

Jesus never made excuses for Himself or for the disciples and their missteps, even when He was in the right or knew their actions would make Him look bad. His posture was to pay attention to what pleased His heavenly Father and what He was called to do—and let the chips fall. If He was maligned, unfairly accused or misunderstood, He didn't say, "Hey, blame My Father. This was all His idea. I was just following orders. Don't kill the messenger."

His Father had ordained, in fact, that they *would* kill the messenger, so Jesus' excuses wouldn't have made a difference anyway. In the same way, perhaps your heavenly Father has ordained that sometimes *you* will be misunderstood for reasons that may not be clear until you see Him face-to-face—and *your* excuses may not make a difference in the outcome either. That may suggest that excuses are to be use sparingly.

Shadrach, Meshach and Abednego demonstrated the same "no excuses" policy as Jesus when King Nebuchadnezzar decided to throw them into the fiery furnace for refusing to bow down to the ninety-foot gold idol he had erected. They made no attempts to explain or excuse their action, probably figuring the king could care less. It's a distinction worth noting because there are times when an explanation *is* called for.

They told the king,

> O Nebuchadnezzar, *we do not need to defend ourselves before you in this matter*. If we are thrown into the

blazing furnace, the God we serve is able to save
us from it, and he will rescue us from your hand,
O king. But even if he does not, we want you to
know, O king, that we will not serve your gods or
worship the image of gold you have set up. (Daniel 3:16-18, emphasis added)

No fudge factor. Their position was unequivocal. God
was capable of sorting out their dilemma. If He didn't, He
must have a good reason. Either way, they didn't try to
avoid the consequences of their decision not to worship the
idol.

If you'd like to steer your life in the direction of less
explaining and fewer excuses, you can start practicing on
God. Excuses are wasted on Him anyway. He already
knows the truth, and He's heard all the explanations—
all the way back to the one about the apple in the Garden. Even then, He knew it wasn't the devil that made
them do it.

Reality

- [ ] Do you frequently make excuses for your behavior?

- [ ] Is there a particular pattern to it—certain situations that trigger the same kind of response from you?

- [ ] What needs to change?

- [ ] Is over-explaining an issue?

- [ ] What are you afraid will happen if you don't explain?

- [ ] While no one is suggesting you never defend yourself, can you think of recent situations where a policy of "no excuses" might have been the better choice?

- [ ] Ask God to teach you when it's appropriate to speak up for yourself and when it's unnecessary.

Let's Make a Deal

The famous tenor Leo Slezak, who often played the lead role in Wagner's opera, *Lohengrin*, loved to tell the story of the night when things backstage didn't go as planned.

There's a moment in the first act of the opera where his character, Lohengrin, is supposed to arrive on stage in a boat drawn by a swan. On this particular night, however, an overly eager stagehand pushed the boat out on stage before Lohengrin was onboard. The tenor, never skipping a beat, turned to the stagehand and asked, "What time does the next swan leave?"

Flexibility is not just a survival skill for opera singers. Flexibility, personally and organizationally, is a critical survival skill in today's rapidly changing marketplace. Some people call it adopting a "judo strategy." Stay nimble, adapt quickly to new requirements or circumstances and leverage the weight of competitors against them.

For most of us, it's a lot more basic. We're trying not to get trampled as the world races into the future.

Two women I interviewed for a *Chicago Tribune* assignment are my nominees for flexibility in action. They were secretaries for a suburban elementary school. They had worked together at adjoining desks for fifteen years, and every day was full of surprises.

During our interview, a third-grader showed up in tears because she forgot her show-and-tell item, a seven-year-old started throwing up because someone told him he could get salmonella poisoning and die from petting his bird. Then there was the parent who insisted little Johnny did not have chicken pox, despite telltale facial blotches. And someone alerted them that the bus company forgot they were supposed to take forty kids on a field trip to the zoo that day. The kids were standing on the curb with their sack lunches, waiting to leave—their five-minute allotment of good behavior totally spent.

According to the secretaries, their biggest challenge came the year the school was completely remodeled over the summer. The project fell behind. The whole school was a mess. The classrooms were stacked from floor to ceiling with desks and chairs. Some days the two women worked with painters standing on their desks.

Just before school started, the principal fell seriously ill. There was no one to spur the project's completion. It looked like school wouldn't open on time. So, the two secretaries sprang into action, enlisting the help of their husbands and kids. They worked every night until midnight through the final weekend putting the school back together. Then they videotaped the entire building and took the tape to the principal's home to assure her that school was ready to open the next day.

"All in a day's work," they claimed. Patience and a sense of humor helped, but flexibility was the key.

I admit that a crisis summons the best in us all, even those who are flexibility-challenged. It's considerably harder to stay flexible in situations where we feel threatened, pushed around or without options. Then, to be flexible feels like we're losing ground. At that point, the natural tendency is to plant our feet, erect a barricade and build a moat for good measure . . . with the bridge always up. No one's going to push *us* around.

The secretaries modeled an alternative approach. The women were decisive, but willing to live with a variety of outcomes. Their bendable-but-not-shakable attitude set a tone that allowed those around them to lighten up too. Their actions communicated that no one had to lose if everyone gave a little.

They accepted that most situations that challenge our flexibility are benign; it's we who make them personal. They understood that everything doesn't have to be a test of who's right or who's in charge. And they didn't waste time trying to negotiate nonnegotiables. Practicing any one of these principles has the potential to lower the stress of almost any situation.

Our relationship with God, on the other hand, requires a whole different kind of flexibility. Have you ever said something to God like, "That commandment about 'Thou shalt not steal' doesn't apply to office supplies I take home from work, does it? After all, I take work home . . . sometimes . . . so that squares things, right? And that thing about tithing? Is that on the gross or the net? Oh, and Your suggestion about getting together with other Christians for worship? Sunday is my only day to golf. How about if I catch a good sermon on the tube? Pretty creative solution, don't you think?"

It sounds like we're trading baseball cards: "I'll trade you two Sammy Sosa cards for one Mark McGwire." We rattle on like street hagglers at a flea market.

God listens, but He doesn't join in. He doesn't "deal." He doesn't negotiate ("You think the Ten Commandments are too hard? Sorry. I'll rework them and get new copy for your approval before the next team meeting.") Instead, He summons us unilaterally to "get with" His program.

Henry Blackaby, in *Knowing and Doing the Will of God*, (part of the *Experiencing God* series), says the second biggest turning point of the Christian life (the first turning point being the decision to choose God) is when we must adjust our lives to God. "You cannot continue life as usual or stay where you are and go with God at the same time," Blackaby says. "Until you are ready to make any adjustment necessary to follow and obey what God has said, you will be of little use to God. Your greatest single difficulty in following God may come at the point of the adjustment."[1]

If you check all the places in the New Testament where Jesus says, "Follow Me," He doesn't invite us to barter with Him for the best deal, just as He doesn't manipulate or intimidate anyone into obedience either.

He makes clear what He expects of His followers (John 12:26). He explains the cost (Matthew 16:24) and the benefits (John 8:12, Matthew 4:19) of adjusting our life to His. He describes the consequences of not adjusting (16:25-26). But in the end, all the bending is done at our end. We are the ones who must choose to adapt. It's another argument for developing a more flexible heart—we'll need it to walk with God.

There's one more benefit to flexibility. It allows God to deploy us quickly into divine opportunities. Besides, unlike the marketplace, with God all the rules will be fair, and there will be wonderful surprises.

☐ How flexible are you? . . . on the job? . . . in personal relationships? . . . in your readiness to adjust to God's claims on your life?

☐ When and where is it hardest to bend?

☐ Why do you think it's an issue?

☐ Ask God to reveal to you a next step in adjusting your plans to His. Invite Him to soften your heart to act quickly and unequivocally to do His bidding.

Managing the "Me" You See

Everybody's heard the story of how Lloyd's of London once insured Betty Grable's legs for a million dollars. In recent years, Lloyd's has insured Bruce Springsteen's voice, the taste buds of renowned food critic Egon Ronay and the bathtub used by a twenty-year-old British navy officer who sailed the tub from England to France. (The officer had to agree to keep the plug in position at all times.) The one thing I've never seen Lloyd's underwrite is someone's reputation. It's a risk not even Lloyd's of London wants to undertake.

Reputation management, impression engineering and corporate positioning are a few of the buzzwords used these days for this art of managing the "me" you see—whether corporate or personal. Sadly, experts say that the truth about us isn't nearly as important as perceptions—what other people *think* we are.

I was asked once to serve briefly as press secretary for a political candidate who was doomed to lose his race because of an unbeatable opponent. The opponent was an incumbent who had been in office forever, had thousands of loyal patronage workers ready to do his bidding and who enjoyed widespread popularity among the voters.

I asked the man who was to be my candidate why he would subject himself to such humiliation, knowing the only question was how badly he would be beaten. He was a decent, honorable guy, and he wasn't stupid.

He replied that he'd spent years in Chicago politics, serving as ward commiteeman, precinct captain, campaign worker—you name it. He did it because his party never backed a candidate who hadn't paid his dues, and someday he wanted to run for the state legislature.

Unfortunately, he blended so well into the organization that he was not perceived as a fighter, a leader or someone capable of capturing the attention of a fickle electorate. In his opinion, the only way he could change their minds was to take on an assignment no one wanted, conduct a credible campaign in the face of insurmountable odds and demonstrate that he was an effective campaigner worth a second look. He then hoped to be slated the following year for a more winnable race as state representative—the post he wanted in the first place. This campaign was not about him or how he stood on the issues. It was about changing everyone's perception of him.

The thing about the reputation police is that they don't really care about *us*. It's all about who we are in relation to everyone else. The goal is for the person, group or entity doing the ranking either to come out on top or hold the key to who comes out on top.

The Pharisees were the reputation management experts of their day. They had hundreds of rules for what it took to be a Pharisee-in-good-standing. They loved pouncing on anyone who didn't qualify.

In John 8, they brought a woman caught in the act of adultery to Jesus and tried to drag Him into a legal debate about how the woman should be punished. They weren't interested in justice, the correct application of the law, the woman or Jesus' answer. They wanted to trap Jesus with His answer and undermine His growing reputation as the possible Messiah. He was messing with their program, getting way too much attention—and doing it without a single image consultant. How rude!

Jesus didn't take the bait—which is a valuable lesson all by itself. Instead, He used an observation and a few targeted questions to reframe the whole discussion. Jesus was like that.

As the Pharisees carried on about the woman, Jesus calmly bent down and started writing something on the ground with His finger. (Do you suppose He was doodling in the dirt the way we doodle on notepads during boring meetings? It's one more reason to love Him.) After the Pharisees had blown off all their steam, Jesus stood up and calmly said, "If any one of you is without sin, let him be the first to throw a stone at her" (8:7).

Basically Jesus said, "Hey, you with the holier-than-thou attitude, take a look in the mirror. It isn't pretty." Unflappable, Jesus waited as the truth soaked in, and the Pharisees slunk away one by one.

Turning to the woman, He gently asked, "Woman, where are they? Has no one condemned you?" (8:10). I don't think He was looking for an answer. The questions simply put the situation in perspective. The Pharisees are not the main problem here, Jesus implied. Your own sin is the problem. It was her turn to look inward.

Then, lest she feel permanently disqualified by her history, Jesus delivered His punchline. "Neither do I condemn you. Go now and leave your life of sin" (8:11).

On the job, among peers, throughout our professional lives, we are constantly measured, ranked and evaluated. Our image and reputation take hits on a daily basis. We can't change that. But we *can* decide not to waste time playing by rules—spoken or unspoken—whose only function is to judge us and put us in someone else's box.

Jesus invites us to take hold of *His* mirror and look inside instead. He won't turn and walk away. He has known who we really are all along. It's OK to face what's good and what's not good about us—to take the forgiveness, freedom from condemnation and restoration He offers.

A new image awaits us. Actually, it's the one that's been there all along, buried behind the facades we use to feel OK about ourselves. It's called the image of Christ.

Reality

☐ What image do you communicate to others? Is it true to who you are?

☐ Do you feel you're unable to be yourself in certain circles because it would not be acceptable? Is it because it would truly be inappropriate or because your life is outside the norms of the group?

☐ Do you like what you see when you look in the mirror?

☐ What do you need forgiveness for or reassurance about?

☐ What would you like people to see in you?

"Can't" — It's Not a Four-Letter Word

I'd rather eat chalk than admit I can't do something. It isn't because I am brimming with self-confidence. It's our culture. Dozens of times a day, in ads on TV and billboards and in newspapers, I'm told I can control my destiny. The U.S. Army tells me to, "be all that you can be." In the blockbuster best-seller, *Bonfire of the Vanities*, Thomas Wolfe claimed we were all "masters of the universe." Like the divine right of kings, we are supposed to be able to do it all. No ceilings allowed.

Martha Stewart has even turned homemaking into an Olympic sport. The domestic-goddess cum one-woman-conglomerate insists that we too can make our very own marshmallows from scratch and roast them over a fire started from twigs whose derivation we know because we've memorized the nomenclature of all plant life while we were packing the picnic basket. Who *is* this woman, and how do I get her out of my house?

The truth is I *can't* do it all—and neither can you. We have limitations.

Sports writers love to repeat the story of how Muhammad Ali would refuse to fasten his seat belt on flights, telling the stewardess, "I don't need a seat belt. I'm Superman!"

"Superman," one stewardess replied, "doesn't need a plane."

The painful awareness that we can't do it all usually comes after a very long time spent trying to prove we can. Then some unpleasant life event slaps us silly.

I have a friend who is a senior executive in one of the nation's top five insurance companies. She feels called to be salt and light in corporate America, and she has been both. In the past two years, in the wake of changing market conditions and stiffer competition, her company has restructured and downsized its workforce three times to stop the hemorrhaging of red ink. Her department has shrunk from seventy-nine employees to six.

"We have limited resources," the company kept saying. "We've got to do more with less." Her sixty-hour workweek ratcheted to seventy hours and counting.

One day, my extremely capable friend looked around her and thought, *You know, I have limited resources too. I need to step back and ask some hard questions about what God wants me to do here.*

Jesus understood limits. Scan any of the gospels and watch as Jesus' ministry exploded at a meteoric rate. See how a poignant healing here and a trenchant teaching there catapulted Him onto a demanding fast track. People clamored for His time and attention. "Over here, Jesus. Say this, Jesus. These 5,000 people need food. That man over there needs his sight. Help them! Hurry! If *You* don't do it, who will?"

It's the kind of clamor heard each day by smart and capable Christians who work hard and want to honor God in all they do. They're in demand. Their employers want them leading the pack because their high values and work ethic are good for business. But the truth is we don't have to do it all.

Jesus didn't heal everybody. He didn't go to every town that wanted Him to pay a visit. He didn't minister nonstop just because the need was great. Sometimes He and the disciples went fishing. Sometimes He went off by Himself to pray. Sometimes He kicked back with friends like Mary, Martha and Lazarus over a good meal. Jesus modeled a life with boundaries.

In Luke, when frazzled Martha was acting like a Martha Stewart wannabe, Jesus explained to her the importance of knowing what we're called to do, of making choices and setting limits.

"You are worried and upset about many things," the Lord told Martha in Luke 10:41-42, "but only one thing is needed. Mary has chosen what is better, and it will not be taken away from her." Mary didn't let outside pressure drive her decisions. She decided what was important and made the tough choice—a choice her own sister did not understand. Jesus applauded her.

Only a few things are necessary for us too. And the person best able to help you identify your few things is not your boss or your kids or your mother. It's Jesus.

Reality

- ☐ Do you know what you are called by God to do and not do at work, at home and in the important relationships of your life?

- ☐ Have you taken on responsibilities that did not belong to you because someone stroked your ego or told you there was no one else to do it?

- ☐ Are you willing to acknowledge your limitations? What are they?

- ☐ What kind of reaction can you expect when you set firmer limits? How can you prepare for it?

Deconstructing the "Mean" Machine

My first job as a young teenager was assisting an elderly couple three times a week after school. I cleaned their house and helped start supper. There wasn't really enough to do for the hours they wanted me at their house because they never messed up anything. But I dusted and re-dusted and mopped and re-mopped so they would feel they received their money's worth. I hated the work, but it paid more than baby-sitting, and teenagers never think they have enough money.

What drove me nuts was the way everything in the house had a place, a very precise place. Perish the thought if I should accidentally set down something in a slightly different place after cleaning it. They claimed it helped them keep track of things. I didn't believe them.

I couldn't picture either of them saying, "Honey, I can't find my pink ceramic ballerina on a pedestal. Do you know where I might have mislaid it?"

"Yes, dear, I think you'll find it three inches from where you left it."

In retrospect, I think it helped them feel safe. As the world grew scarier and more complex, it was comforting to them, I guess, to have as many things as possible locked into place.

I used to think they were unusual until I became an adult and noticed how we put other people into slots and lock them in place all the time. We form an attitude toward an entire group of people based on the actions of a few and, at its ugliest, it turns into war and other acts of violence. How smart is that?

Prejudice affects behavior at both ends of the experience, even if it doesn't reach the level of violence. Author Philip Yancey says that as a teenager he went to elaborate lengths to change his speech, his behavior and even his handwriting to erase any trace of his Southern upbringing. He didn't want to be pigeonholed as a hillbilly.

"Since the rest of the nation in the 1960s seemed to judge Southerners as backward, ignorant and racist," he says, "I wanted to disassociate myself from my region."[1]

Prejudice feels different when it's personal. When I was a full-time reporter, I covered many bitter labor strikes—everyone from firefighters to teachers to autoworkers. I watched people who had worked together for years turn against each other because one of them crossed a picket line and stepped out of his assigned slot to identify himself with his striking coworkers.

As one "scab" told me as he walked past his union brothers into the plant, "You know, when the plant shuts down, and they turn out the lights, we all look the same in the dark." Not everyone saw it that way.

In this country, we legislate against prejudice when it affects a person's ability to find work or housing. But legislation doesn't change anyone's mind and heart. Only God can do that.

About a year and a half ago, I began meeting with an African-American woman in my church. We had similar interests; we were both professionals working on major career decisions. We decided to get together periodically to pray for one other. In the process, a friendship developed.

As we shared the events of our lives over the next several months, I was struck by how much harder she, as a black woman, had to work to ensure she would have the opportunity to get *onto* the so-called level playing field.

"You know the proverb about, 'If you keep your mouth closed, people will think you're wise'? " she said. "Well, if your skin color is different, you can walk in the door and get points knocked off before you've ever opened your mouth. I don't need to go back 200 years to find prejudice. I can go back twenty minutes." And she had the stories to prove it.

She told me about agreeing to house-sit for white friends who live in a very exclusive neighborhood. She asked them to inform the neighbors why she was there and to write a note which she could carry with her because "when people see a black person in a home in that neighborhood, they assume the only reason she's there is to clean it or steal from it."

She travels internationally in her job. Her travels, she says, have reinforced her belief that mankind's core problem is not racism or sexism or ageism or any other "ism." It's hate in the human heart.

"I recently returned from Russia," she told me. "The Russians hate the gypsies. Lithuanians hate the Russians. In Sudan, blacks hate other blacks—Muslims against Christians. It really proves what Scripture says—that we don't wrestle against flesh and blood but against the powers of darkness. Sometimes the darkest corner of the world is in our hearts."

The apostle Peter struggled with prejudice. It had more to do with religious discrimination than any other kind of prejudice, but the end result was the same.

In Acts 10, God used a vision and a centurion to change Peter's mind about the Gentiles, whom Peter didn't believe could be on the same footing with God as the Jews.

In the vision God started working on Peter's heart by commanding him to eat food that Gentiles ate—food forbidden to Jews by rabbinical law. Peter objected. Three times the heavenly voice had to tell Peter it was a mistake to call anything unclean that God had made clean. It was a short leap from food to people. It's also wrong to call people inferior when God doesn't.

The Holy Spirit then told Peter to expect Gentile visitors, emissaries sent by Cornelius. The centurion, the Bible says, was a "devout and God-fearing Gentile" (Acts 10:2) who wanted Peter to come and teach him "everything the Lord has commanded you to tell us" (10:33).

Now Peter *really* had a problem. Rabbinical law forbade Jews from associating with Gentiles, much less accepting their hospitality. But how could he refuse? Cornelius was hungry to know more about God, and God had commanded Peter to go.

When Peter and Cornelius finally met and Peter began to preach to Cornelius and his assembled friends, Peter admitted how God had changed his heart about the Gentiles. "I now realize how true it is that God does not show favoritism, but accepts men from every nation who fear him and do what is right" (10:34-35).

Then Peter shared how Christ died on the cross to pay the sin debt we owed to a Holy God, how God raised Christ from the dead to demonstrate how He had conquered death and how "*everyone* who believes in him receives forgiveness of sins through his name" (10:43, emphasis added). Everyone!

In God's eyes there's only one category of people—sinner. We're all in that category until we accept His gift of forgiveness. Then we become *forgiven* sinners—not female sinners or disabled sinners or Southern sinners or African-American sinners.

There will be no minorities in heaven. We can give people a taste of heaven by treating them that way now.

Reality

☐ Have you personally experienced some form of prejudice? How did you feel?

☐ Have you ever discriminated against an individual or group? Would you describe it as a careless action or a deliberate effort to put someone in his or her place?

☐ Think about what it would be like to live next door to such people in heaven for all eternity. Do you need to discuss it with God?

The Ultimate Put-Down

A pop culture pundit in an essay in a national magazine recently declared the death of politically correct language. I don't know if his supply of euphemisms was running low or if he just got tired of being sensitive, but I don't expect a major change in public behavior anytime soon. People are getting too much mileage out of distorting PC language. Take rejection, which in today's culture has been raised to the level of an artform.

A fifty-seven-year old man loses his job as senior vice president of a chemical company. The company says they need someone more "globally nimble" with "relevant" experience—his twenty-plus years of superior performance and loyalty apparently not counting as relevant.

An old college chum calls to say her husband walked out because he was ready for an "encore marriage."

An airline spokesperson talks to reporters about a "disruption risk" (a strike). A corporate executive describes a "labor allocation adjustment" (layoffs).

Is any of this supposed to hurt less because it's been dressed up in party clothes? That's ridiculous. The truth is, rejection hurts. It's a loss. It changes everything.

At some point we have to learn what to do with rejection. I'm not talking about how to recover from the circumstances it creates. Leave that to the therapists. Nor how to avoid rejection. You'll have more luck avoiding the wind. But we need to learn how to handle what it does to our hearts.

Developing a thicker skin is the normal fallback position, but numbing our hearts has the same effect as a carbon monoxide leak. You can't see or smell what's happening, but eventually it kills you. When we can't feel our own pain, our ability to feel the pain of others goes out the window too. It's like systematically stamping out what is supposed to mark us as children of God—the ability to love wholeheartedly in spite of being rejected.

God felt firsthand the pain of rejection from the children of Israel. They were so fickle and outrageous in how they repeatedly thumbed their noses at Him that most of us would have written them off early on. But He had made a promise to be their God. Their lack of commitment didn't change His commitment. It was an "in-spite-of" rather than a "because-of" kind of love.

First, He expressed disappointment. He described His hurt. Then, because He is a holy God who will not be mocked, sometimes His anger burned hot, and He turned His back for a season to show the Israelites the barrenness of life without Him. But never, never, never did He completely forsake them.

It's hard to imagine God with hurt feelings. If you run the entire universe and you're Perfect, Complete, Omnipotent, Eternal, doesn't it follow that you wouldn't care if someone rejected you? Who needs *them*?

That's the point. He doesn't *need* us. He *loves* us. It's precisely because we *matter* to Him that our rejection hurts Him so much. Nevertheless, He perseveres.

> "For a brief moment I abandoned you,
>   but with deep compassion I will bring you
>   back.
> In a surge of anger
>   I hid my face from you for a moment,
> but with everlasting kindness
> I will have compassion on you," says the LORD
> your Redeemer. (Isaiah 54:7-8)

> "Though the mountains be shaken
>   and the hills be removed,
> yet my unfailing love for you will not
>   be shaken
> nor my covenant of peace be removed,"
> says the LORD, who has compassion on you.
> (54:10)

No dead heart here. He keeps loving like it's never going to hurt.

If you want to avoid being hurt again, you'll have to lock yourself in your room and spend the rest of your life writing stories that turn out the way you'd like. Rejection goes with the territory. A barricaded heart simply cuts you off from ever receiving the love and compassion you're looking for. We are called, instead, to keep our hearts tender, free of bitterness and fully operational.

To tell God you can't or won't trust again or love again or be vulnerable again because you have been wounded is to tell God He isn't big enough to protect you and heal your pain. Telling Him what He *can't* do is just as offensive as telling Him what He *must* do to make you happy.

He's enough. Let Him love your heart out of hiding. Then maybe we can turn the words, "I feel your pain," into something besides a comedian's punch line. After all, showing love and compassion was never supposed to be a laughing matter.

Reality

☐ How big a role has rejection played in your life? At work? With friends? With family?

☐ Have you "owned" your hurt and processed how it has affected you, or have you simply ignored it and moved on?

☐ How do you typically handle rejection—both on the giving and receiving end?

☐ What would you like to do differently in the future?

☐ Talk to God about it.

When the Odds Don't Matter

We live in an era of unprecedented risk-taking by men and women of all ages. One of the more startling recreational trends in America is the extreme sport of BASE jumping. The acronymic name refers to the four types of structures which BASE jumpers leap from—Buildings, Antennas, Spans (bridges) and Earth (cliffs). They use rectangular canopy chutes and toggles for steering, but, unlike skydivers, carry no reserve parachute. Their heart-stopping, double-dare- you actions scream, "OK, world! Look at me! I'm here!" The price for this ultimate rush is one of the highest fatality rates in the sporting world.

Most of us will never come remotely close to taking that kind of risk. Real life is scary enough. Still, we admire people who come off the sidelines and jump into life with a "take-no-prisoners" boldness, who put it all on the line to prove something.

Not all risk is equal. In the business world, what often passes for risk-taking is so calculated, measured and hedged

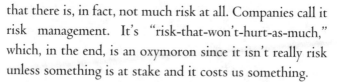

that there is, in fact, not much risk at all. Companies call it risk management. It's "risk-that-won't-hurt-as-much," which, in the end, is an oxymoron since it isn't really risk unless something is at stake and it costs us something.

I think one of the gutsiest women in the Bible is the prostitute in Luke 7:36-47. We don't know her name, and we never hear about her again after her story plays out. All we know is that somewhere along the line she heard Jesus preach about forgiveness of sins, and it rocked her world. Could it be true? Could her slate truly be wiped clean? If it were true—really true—she was willing to risk everything to acknowledge such love.

She found Jesus dining at the home of a Pharisee named Simon. Her presence was not forbidden since it was common for outsiders to observe and listen to the conversations of those more learned.

Her plan was to slip in behind Jesus and pour a jar of expensive perfume over His feet as He reclined on His side next to a low table piled with food. It was a simple, humble gesture—to wash the dust of the day off Jesus' feet. She didn't plan to talk to Him. She didn't expect Him to look her in the eye or give her any individual attention. She just wanted to show Him how grateful she was for His unspeakable gift.

The boldness of her plan once on the scene, however, was totally unacceptable behavior for a woman of her dubious reputation. Even though she didn't plan to draw attention to herself, she was, after all, pond scum. Still, she pressed on. Christ *had* to know of her love and appreciation.

Something happened when she got close enough to Jesus to touch His feet. Before she could even open the bottle of perfume, involuntarily she began to weep a torrent of grateful tears. It was Him—Jesus—right under her fingertips. Being that close to Jesus can do that to a person.

Her tears soaked His feet and she—well, let's just say she was a mess, sobbing and crumpled in a heap at Jesus' feet, runny nose and all.

She didn't care. For one shining moment, it didn't matter what people thought. Not that day. Public censure? Humiliation? So what. She had lost her self-respect long ago. Jesus was the first person who offered to return it. What mattered was to love Jesus extravagantly and to take His gift of forgiveness.

Have you ever loved Jesus like that? On the job or in the presence of unbelieving friends or out in your community, has it ever been important to put it all on the line for Him regardless of what it might cost?

Jesus honored her commitment. He held her up before the assembled crowd as an example of the best kind of love. And, in one subtle gesture, He gave her dignity. Luke 7:44 says, "Then he [Jesus] turned toward the woman and said to Simon, 'Do you see this woman? I came into your house. You did not give me any water for my feet, but she wet my feet with her tears and wiped them with her hair.' "

How curious! Even though Jesus' pointed remarks were directed to Simon, *He looked at the woman* as He spoke. She didn't need to hover behind Jesus with eyes cast downward, slinking in the shadows in shame, not making eye contact. Jesus looked her squarely in the eye as if to say, "I'm honored by your love. It's My joy to forgive your sins and acknowledge such faith. Hold your head high. You're a different woman now."

With Jesus, forgiveness is never a transaction. It's personal. He didn't come to earth just to clear up a sin problem. He came to change the way we feel about ourselves and give us back our dignity. He looks us straight in the eye and tells us things are different now. He'll even draw as close as our fingertips if we're willing to take the risk.

Reality

- [ ] What's the biggest risk you've ever taken in life?

- [ ] How does it compare to the biggest risk you've ever taken spiritually?

- [ ] What's the riskiest thing you can imagine God asking you to do in the life you're now living?

- [ ] Are you a little afraid of getting that intimately involved with Him?

- [ ] Ask Him to meet you where you are and show you how to relate to Him more deeply.

Riding the Edge of Normal

One of my favorite children's books is *Alexander and the Terrible, Horrible, No Good, Very Bad Day* by Judith Viorst. Stress is hardly the exclusive domain of kids. In the workplace we marinate in it. We just call it something else.

If the company's stock takes a beating, they call it "a brief episode of inhibited performance." What they really mean is, "Things didn't turn out as planned. Our company is having a terrible, horrible, no good, very bad day."

Companies survive. They fire the VP whose brilliant idea took the company into the tank and hastily announce "bold new initiatives" to turn things around. To hear them tell it, you'd think it was planned that way all along. Wouldn't it be nice if we could do the same thing with the stress in our personal lives?

Life does not take note of our distress and graciously uncomplicate itself. We can't fire our boss, downsize the kids when they misbehave or reengineer nasty people off our church committees. There are no spin doctors to make our mistakes sound like valuable research.

In his book *Yearning*, Craig Barnes says, "It threatens us to the core of our being to think that we are subject to the same laws of nature as the dead dog on the side of the road." That's why, he says, we work hard to prove we're not limited by our circumstances and not hampered by anything but puny dreams. He calls it "a beautiful lie."[1]

Several years ago, *Good Health* magazine published an article on the connection between stress and illness. The article included a self-assessment test developed by Dr. Thomas H. Holmes, a psychiatrist at the University of Washington in Seattle. Forty-three types of emotional stress—including several which were job-related—were ranked in order of severity and given a numeric value. You could tally your total stress (which itself should have been listed as Stress #44) and assess your likelihood of getting sick in the near future.[2]

I agree that it's a good idea to understand the consequences of the heavy loads we carry. Living healthy lifestyles and not abusing our bodies are ways we honor God. Still, I keep thinking, *What if people can't change their circumstances? What about the single mom with three kids in a low-paying job and no extended family nearby to help out, what then?* Those stresses aren't going away anytime soon.

King Jehoshaphat faced this decision in Second Chronicles 20 when the dreaded Moabites and Ammonites declared war on Judah. He couldn't do anything about the circumstances. He and his people were clearly in over their heads.

He made an important decision. He brought everyone together in an atmosphere of fasting, community and prayer and turned everyone's attention away from the crisis and toward God.

- *They acknowledged that God was ultimately the One in charge of their circumstances.* "You rule over all the kingdoms of the nations. Power and might are in your hand, and no one can withstand you" (20:6).

- *They recalled God's past faithfulness.* "O our God, did you not drive out the inhabitants of this land before your people Israel and give it forever to the descendants of Abraham your friend?" (20:7).

- *They admitted their total dependence on Him for the outcome.* "For we have no power to face this vast army that is attacking us. We do not know what to do, but our eyes are upon you" (20:12).

- *God encouraged them to hang on.* "This is what the LORD says to you: 'Do not be afraid or discouraged because of this vast army. For the battle is not yours, but God's'" (20:15).

- *They faced their challenge head-on.* The next day, in spite of their fears, they marched off to confront their enemy. God set an ambush between the enemy armies. By the time Jehoshaphat and his men showed up, the two enemy armies had killed each other. The battle was over. Peace fell on the land and not one of God's people had to draw a sword.

Keeping our eyes on God instead of circumstances is not a *last* option. It's the *best* option. Circumstances do our bidding only occasionally. With God, though, it's a different story. He never has a terrible, horrible, no good, very bad day. No doors slam in *His* face. The doors, the keys and the house belong to Him.

I want to live in His house.

Reality

☐ What are the biggest stresses in your life?

☐ Are there things you can do to change these circumstances?

☐ What part of your situation is not likely to change anytime soon?

☐ Has your attitude helped or hindered your ability to face this?

☐ What would you do differently if your eyes were consistently on God and not on your difficulties?

The Brass Ring Thing

*H*ow will you know if your life has been a success? What will you have done during the hyphen between the years of your birth and death? Will the yardstick be the size of your bank account? The respect of peers? The achievements cataloged on a stunning résumé? Well-adjusted children?

It's easier to know what we *don't* want. We don't want to be poor, hungry, alone, ignored. We don't want a meaningless life. We want to know that our fourscore-and-ten years made a difference. How to ensure that end is less clear. People have midlife crises because they see the finish line in view and still haven't figured it out.

The most common way we define success is through our job. Parents communicate to kids early on that "if you want to make something of yourself," you'll be a teacher or a doctor or a fill-in-your-family's-definition-of-choice. The key, Mom and Dad say, is to get the best job possible and be really, really good at it.

We start asking kids in elementary school, "What do you want to be when you grow up?" Kids know better than to answer, "I've decided to be a really fun person with a killer tennis backhand and a talent for putting people at ease." Dad is likely to say, "Son, tell that to a mortgage broker and see how far it gets you. That won't put food on the table." Kids know the real question is, "What are you going to do when you grow up?" They instinctively sense it needs to be an important job that provides significant money, recognition and other rewards if the adults are to approve.

So, at eighteen we set off for college and make a career choice with less self-knowledge, wisdom and work experience than we will ever have the rest of our life. By the time we figure out that getting a job is not the same as getting a life, our course is set. Momentum pulls us along.

Years later, when frustration, dissatisfaction and fatigue tell us something is wrong, it feels like it's too late to do anything about it. We can't pick up and join the circus. There's a spouse, kids, mortgage and car payment! It's further complicated by the fact that we've picked up the trappings of success along the way—and we're used to them.

But, if this is success, what's all this yearning about? If I'm doing so well, why do I feel so bad?

Maybe our definition of success is wrong.

When I was in broadcasting, I occasionally participated in charity events such as TV telethons to benefit disease research or the annual fund-raising telethon for public television. Telethon producers would round up as many media types as possible to answer phones or hand out checks on camera. Most were TV news anchors with recognizable faces—the thought being that they would attract viewers who would then pledge beaucoup bucks to the cause. Because I worked for a major network affiliate, occasionally we radio types were pressed into service.

During one particular event, I was standing off-camera, waiting to be told what to do. It happened during a season in my life when I was trying to figure out what success looked like for me and whether I had achieved it.

A twenty-something junior producer came over to me, clipboard in hand, and looked me up and down with obvious disdain. He scanned his list of celebrity guests, then looked up and said, "Are you anybody?"

My mouth dropped open in disbelief. "Well . . . no . . . I'm not *any*body," I said and then burst out laughing. "In fact, I used to be *no*body. Does that help you? But listen," I whispered, leaning toward him, "now I'm *somebody*—just not somebody you know." He shook his head and walked away.[1]

That clinched it. I didn't want to play anymore by someone else's definition of success. There had to be a different way. Colossians 2:20 gave me courage: "Since you died with Christ to the basic principles of this world, why, as though you still belonged to it, do you submit to its rules?" Time to change the rules.

How does God define a well-lived life? Ephesians 2:10 says, "We are God's workmanship, created in Christ Jesus to do good works, which God prepared in advance for us to do." When God made us, He put together a total package—a life plan—that would give us all the satisfaction and meaning we could stand. But we have to understand it's much bigger than a mere job description. And we have to take the time to figure out what it will look like for us.

Tom Paterson in his book, *Living the Life You Were Meant to Live*, says, "Life is not about making a living, but about *living*. For Christians, a career is not about money, but about fulfilling our calling. It is about seeing our work as ministry and about using our giftedness to bring glory to God on the earth."[2]

Our job is to identify the gifts and talents and passions God stamped on our DNA and *be* that person—wherever God places us. What we *do* will cascade out of it. Paterson says we're not guaranteed a life of ease, but it will fit. There will be an absence of psychological and emotional chafing. Whatever we do won't feel like work.

For too much of my life I obsessed over whether I was in the right job or in the right career. Belatedly, I've realized my deepest satisfaction came when I was doing certain things that flowed out of who I am—for example, anything creative, anything that allows me to lead, influence and motivate others to action, anything that requires critical thinking skills and problem-solving, anything that allows me to build a bridge between different people—regardless of the context.

The clues were there all along. They showed up when I sold Girl Scout cookies as a child, ran for student council in high school, wrote an on-the-road newsletter while traveling for nine months with a Christian music group, disciplined my child, decorated my home, served as a product manager for a manufacturer, went undercover to do a TV story on child prostitution, led a small group at church, rallied neighbors to get our sidewalks repaired. It also explains why I hated certain jobs, despite their good salary and attractive perks. I kept wanting my occupation to define what constituted a life worth living. But my occupation was never big enough to hold all the satisfaction and meaning God wanted to give my life.

There's nothing wrong with wanting a meaningful job and wanting to be really, really good at it. But don't stop looking for the *life* with your name on it.

Reality

☐ What would your life look like if it really turned out well?

☐ Is it dependent on a particular job or title?

☐ What do you know about yourself that's a clue to how God "wrapped" you?

☐ Is there opportunity to use those gifts in your current occupation?

☐ What next steps are appropriate to live more fully the life with your name on it?

Hampered by the "Hurry" Sickness

For most of my life I've been the Queen of Hurry. Valiantly I would sharpen my organizational skills and implement the latest time management techniques. It never netted more margin—just room for additional things to creep onto my calendar. Time became an enemy to be wrestled to the ground. Relentlessly, the clock made its demands and most days the clock won.

I woke up one day facing midlife, dissatisfied and depleted. I wasn't sure what was wrong, but I knew that if I kept *it* up, *it* would kill me.

Actually, time was only part of the problem. In a radical effort to find answers, I quit my job and began the tedious process of reclaiming my life. During that season, I took a forty-day trip alone on America's back roads—with my family's blessing—thinking, praying, journaling and talking to ordinary people about their lives.

In a tiny town in rural Kentucky, I met a man they called Duck Man. He had lived "up north" in Indiana before a brain tumor and subsequent surgery forced him to give up his job as a machinist. He moved his family to Kentucky to start over.

He went through an awful depression. All he knew how to be was a machinist. To fight the blackness, every day he went down to the Cadiz River to feed the ducks. The ducks asked nothing of him. They gratefully accepted his gift of corn and stale bread and gave him an audience as he poured out his heart and tried to figure out what his life was now to be about.

Over time, the number of ducks who showed up at his "table" grew, as did stories of the tender care he gave them. The media caught wind of it, and a Louisville TV station sent a camera crew to track him down. CNN picked up the story. Eventually people started showing up from all over the country, looking for the man who found meaning and peace in the simple act of serving the ducks along the Cadiz River.

I asked him why he thought folks sought him out.

"Most folks have the 'hurry sickness,'" he said. "They don't know where they're going, but they have to get there fast. They must think the answer is up ahead, and they have to beat everybody else to it."

The truth of his words hit with such force that he might as well have punched me in the stomach. Even my sabbatical had been filled with lists for managing my leisure, schedules to make every moment count and a sense of being constantly in motion. What is our rush? Are we racing to cram enough into our lives for them to add up to something, hoping in the end that it will be "enough"?

I wonder if we also rush because we feel so needy. In simpler times, food, shelter and gainful employment were all most people expected from life. Today, though, we expect much more, and we're confused about "wants" and "needs."

We *want* comfort, financial security, status, power, affirmation, significance and intimacy. We *want* to be entertained and challenged. But we chase them down so aggressively, we act like our very life is at stake if we don't get them. We *need* them to survive and be happy—or at least we think we do.

Time is supposed to be our handmaiden in this need-meeting marathon. It's the basket into which we place all the people, places and things that will help us get what we want. When the basket is not big enough, we end up disappointed and exhausted, insisting everything would have been fine if we just had more time.

USA Today once reported, tongue-in-cheek, how much time it would take in a day to live an excellent life—to be successful on the job, to be physically fit, engage in healthy relationships, grow intellectually and contribute to the world around us. They calculated it would take a forty-two-hour day.

Did God miscalculate? No. If He created a day with twenty-four hours, then that's exactly how much time we need to do what He placed us here to do. The problem is not insufficient time. The problem is how we view it and what we do with it. Time was never supposed to enslave us. It is a way of organizing human experience so everything didn't happen all at once.

We ask more from time than it can deliver. In Psalm 90, the psalmist said we can expect seventy or eighty years if we are healthy—and some of those years will bring trouble and sorrow. Suddenly, our time is up, and we disappear. *"Teach us to use wisely all the time we have.* Help us, LORD! Don't wait! Pity your servants. When morning comes, *let your love satisfy all our needs.* Then we can celebrate and be glad for what time we have left" (90:12-14, CEV, emphasis added).

It's not our calendar that needs whipping into shape. It's understanding the difference between wants and needs and knowing where to go to get them met. God is our Need Meeter. If we allow Him to reshape our thinking, we'll know what to pick up and what to lay down. Some of the things we do to feel OK about our lives won't be necessary. There will be room again on our calendars for sanity and margin.

The payoff, the psalmist suggests, is that we will be able to live our remaining days on the earth satisfied, unshackled by the tyranny of the urgent. We can enjoy time and spend it doing what God puts in our hand to do. We might even discover that God's idea of a twenty-four-hour day was "just right."

Reality

- [ ] Are you effectively managing the pace of your life? If not, what is the main reason things are out of control?

- [ ] Are you ready to eliminate hurry from your life?

- [ ] Look at your schedule and think carefully about how much of your time goes toward wants and how much goes toward needs. Has there been confusion between the two?

- [ ] Are some of your activities filling a hole that God Himself wants to fill? Talk it over with Him.

PART THREE:

Spiritual Flashpoints

What's Wrong with Doing It My Way?

Not long ago I interviewed a woman for a story assignment for the *Chicago Tribune*. Afterward, she invited me out for coffee, and our conversation turned personal. She described a freak accident that took her husband's life three years earlier.

Early one cold winter morning, Bob left home for his daily four-mile run in a nearby forest preserve. A fresh dusting of snow that morning concealed the solid sheet of ice that had formed overnight on the paved bike path. Her husband was a tall man. When he hit an icy patch, his feet went out from under him, and he landed with brutal force squarely on his back.

Forest preserve workers rushed to his aid and argued over how best to transport him to a hospital, but Bob would hear nothing of it. No hospital. "I'm an athlete—I know my body," he told them emphatically. "Just get me home. I'll take a pain pill and spend the day in bed. I'll be fine."

At home, his wife begged him to get checked out by a doctor. He steadfastly refused. Thirty-six hours later, his body functions began to shut down. An ambulance rushed him to a nearby hospital where doctors confirmed that he had severed his spinal cord. He never left the hospital. And he died ten months later.

"Why wouldn't he see a doctor?" I asked with astonishment.

"You don't understand," she said. "Bob never listened to anybody. He always had to do things *his* way."

I still shake my head in disbelief at Bob's story, but who am I kidding? I do the same thing in the spiritual realm when it comes to taking the counsel of other Christians. Sometimes I'm willing. Sometimes I'm not. I know it's an important protection provided for us by God, but I don't always enjoy it. Taking the counsel of others, I think, is about the toughest part of living in the family of God.

I often ask friends who are new Christians what is the biggest obstacle to their moving beyond their initial salvation experience to the life of a fully devoted Christ-follower. What usually comes out is some variation of, "I don't want somebody telling me what to do. I want to be the only one who decides what's best for me."

It's odd. We're held accountable every day in other areas of our lives, and we don't have a coronary over it. We don't get to drive any speed we want. We can't ignore

IRS tax laws. On the job, there are quotas, goals, performance evaluations—all requiring us to meet standards set by others. Those who own their own companies have creditors, customers and vendors who have expectations of them. So why do we get bent out of shape when God asks us to help each other grow using the guidelines established in His policy manual, the Bible?

I can think of three reasons for resistance right off the bat: 1) our past experience with accountability has soured us, 2) we don't understand its upside and 3) we're not good at it and have no incentive to improve. Any one of the three is enough to send most of us running.

In their *Pursuing Spiritual Transformation* Bible study series, John Ortberg, Judson Poling and Laurie Pederson describe two types of people we can run into on our spiritual journey. There are the Truth Inflicters who are quick to confront but short on love and compassion. And there are the Truth Avoiders who pretend everything is hunky dory rather than disturb the status quo.[1] Operating at either extreme can leave one or both parties hurt, ignored, wary and more (i.e., "Let's not do *that* again.").

There's a good working model for mutual accountability in Exodus 18 where Jethro helped his son-in-law Moses work through a serious management problem.

Part of Moses' job as he led more than a million people around in the wilderness was to settle everyone's disputes. It was exhausting work. You'd think he would have come up with a better system, but maybe he had a blind spot. We all have them. It's one reason we need a buddy system.

The incident shows a healthy give-and-take between two people who each want God's best. The Bible says Moses and Jethro loved each other and showed it. Moses shared openly about what was going on in his life (18:7-8). Jethro and Moses celebrated successes and praised God for His faithfulness (18:10-12). Jethro cared about Moses' life. He watched how Moses interacted with people and reported what he saw and how it appeared to be affecting Moses.

Love, honesty, openness, affirmation, a guarded tongue, listening without attacking, offering constructive feedback. Sounds like a plan.

In Exodus 18:17-19, Jethro suggested a solution to Moses' problem. "What you are doing is not good," he says. "You and these people who come to you will only wear yourselves out. The work is too heavy for you; you cannot handle it alone. Listen now to me and I will give you some advice."

Jethro suggested Moses redistribute the work to trusted colleagues, leaving Moses to handle only the most difficult cases. Jethro reminded Moses of the payoff: "You will be able to stand the strain, and all these people will go home satisfied" (18:23). The Bible says Moses listened to Jethro and took his advice. Jethro dispensed both truth and grace—especially grace. Moses demonstrated a willingness to act on the truth. Everybody won.

Spiritual accountability is not optional. Jesus modeled it during His earthly ministry. He never made a major decision without talking it over with His Father. True, God gave us the Bible and the Holy Spirit to help us. But the body of Christ around us is our horizontal reality check.

"Therefore confess your sins to each other and pray for each other so that you may be healed" (James 5:16). "As iron sharpens iron, so one man sharpens another" (Proverbs 27:17).

God doesn't need us to keep score on our brothers' and sisters' behavior. He already knows the score. He'd probably be happy, though, to have us act like we're His kids and glad to be in the same family. The whole point of a family, after all, is that no one goes through life alone.

Reality

☐ What has been your experience with accountable relationships?

☐ If something painful happened, what went wrong?

☐ Are you a Truth Inflicter or Truth Avoider?

☐ Are you ready to take off the mask and take a stab at being accountable to at least one trusted, mature Christian friend?

About Those Mattress Warning Labels . . .

They say character is who you are when no one is looking. Does removing mattress warning labels count against me? When I was a little kid I couldn't wait to grow up so I could rip off those puppies with reckless abandon. Sleeping each night atop dire warnings, WHICH ARE ALWAYS WRITTEN IN CAPITAL LETTERS TO SHOW THEY MEAN BUSINESS, felt like sleeping over a nuclear silo. What if I accidentally ripped off a tag while thrashing around in my sleep? I was certain I'd end up deader than Elvis.

Everyone wants to be seen as a person of good character, but what exactly does that mean? How do you know if you have "the right stuff" and enough of it? I've heard people say that going through a crisis forms character. In my experience, crisis reveals character; it doesn't build it.

Character is the sum of all the moral qualities and traits that make up our nature. It's the truest picture of who we are right now, based on all the choices we've made so far. It colors how we see things which, in turn, determines how we will act in the future.

Does that make character the chicken or the egg? Do good choices develop good character? Or does good character determine good choices? The real question is who or what is shaping our choices (and, thus, our character) at both ends of the equation.

One of the first things you learn as a reporter is to check the legitimacy of sources. If your sources aren't credible, the end product will be flawed. Garbage in, garbage out. A favorite mantra at Chicago's now-defunct City News Bureau, where many famous journalists got their start, was, "If your mother says she loves you, check it out."

There's a second axiom journalists learn—usually the hard way. It's based on the scientific principle that nature abhors a vacuum. When a news story is unfolding and no answers or information are forthcoming by those involved, the public (and, some would say, the media) will rush in with a judgment of their own to fill the void. It may be the wrong judgment, but the vacuum demands content.

Both principles apply to the development of character. When you make choices, what sources do you draw from? Are they worthy and credible guides to character development? If you've never really given it much thought except in vague generalities, are you, by inaction, letting other people shape your character with content that has a decidedly different aroma?

Your character is being shaped every day by something—God, the people around you, what you read, where you go, what your eyes see, what you listen to—whether you're proactive in the process or not. Ephesians 5:15-16 says, "Be very careful, then, how you live—not as unwise but as wise, making the most of every opportunity, because the days are evil." It's a call to vigilance in an area where it's easy to skate.

Scripture is full of suggestions for character development. But many of the promises are conditional, dependent on our choices. *If* you do thus and so, *then* thus and so will happen. Proverbs chapter 2 is typical:

> *If* you accept my words
>   and store up my commands within you,
> turning your ear to wisdom
>   and applying your heart to understanding,
> and *if* you call out for insight
>   and cry aloud for understanding,
> and *if* you look for it as for silver
>   and search for it as for hidden treasure. . . .
> *Then* you will understand what is right and just
>   and fair—every good path.
> For wisdom will enter your heart,
>   and knowledge will be pleasant to your soul.
> Discretion will protect you,
>   and understanding will guard you. (2:1-4,
> 9-11, emphasis added)

Character development is not a spectator sport. We have to be a player if we want to affect the end result.

In researching a story on the impact of Christians on public school reform, I learned that the Chicago public school system, the second largest in the nation, has incorporated character education into its curriculum. At every grade level, educators teach ten basic values, including respect, honesty, responsibility and so on. They say kids aren't learning about character and values at home anymore, as evidenced by a generation of children who are more violent than ever before.

Dr. Janette Wilson, a lawyer, ordained Baptist minister and former executive director of Operation PUSH, now works for the school system as director of the Interfaith Community Partnership. Wilson got involved in bringing character education into the schools after attending thirty-three funerals of children while at PUSH. She described the story of eleven-year-old "Yummy" Sandifer, who in 1994 murdered another child and then in turn was killed by gang members.

At Yummy's funeral, Wilson said, "The kids were counting the limousines of the politicians who came. They were admiring the fact that Yummy made the cover of TIME, even though all he'd done was kill somebody and be killed."[1]

Somewhere along the line, their young characters had already begun to take shape. They were already making choices about what was true and not true, what was valuable and not valuable—choices that set them on a path that would likely lead them to a fate similar to Yummy's.

In 1994 we could all sit back and say Yummy's problem was an inner-city problem. That was before Columbine and Jonesboro and Dallas and Atlanta—the list is now so long we don't keep track of locations anymore.

Character doesn't show up on your doorstep and say "I want to live here." You have to want it—want it as much as those little kids who were willing to kill in order to make the cover of *TIME* magazine.

Reality ✓

- ☐ Do you believe it's necessary to be active in your own character development, or do you believe it's something God shapes as you normally mature?

- ☐ How would you describe the state of your character?

- ☐ What is your basis for decision-making?

- ☐ Are there activities or people you have felt in the past were benign but which, upon reflection, may be tainting your character reservoir?

Unleashing the Power of "We"

For years, the American ideal of community meant close extended family members who lived under the same roof and neighbors who had lived next door to us forever. We knew the name of everyone on the block and attended everyone's school play, wedding, baby dedication and funeral. But families don't stick together like they used to.

According to *U.S. News & World Report*, only about forty percent of American families are now traditional two-parent households. Grandma and Grandpa live in a condo in Florida, and Junior shares a loft in another city with assorted friends and strangers. We move so often we may never meet the neighbors. Yesterday's communities are now described in museum exhibits as a twentieth-century historic phenomena.[1]

What hasn't changed is our desire to belong. Since we don't necessarily find a sense of belonging anymore at home or in our neighborhoods, the modern workplace has picked up the "community" baton. Collaboration and teamwork are hot concepts in the marketplace. They link our need to feel connected with an employer's need for a more committed workforce.

Have you noticed that we no longer work in an "office" with "coworkers?" We work on "teams" with "colleagues" or "collaborators." Executive performance reviews not only evaluate individual achievement; they measure how a person contributed to the success of the team. In fact, from time to time, companies spend enormous sums of money on professionally led team-building events.

During my years in corporate middle management, I once spent a day with fellow managers participating in an outdoor experiential challenge course—a sort of boot camp for executives, lead by trained masochists (OK, they were actually corporate trainers). We climbed walls, walked across horizontal rope ladders twenty feet off the ground and performed other feats of daring to learn to work cooperatively.

Our team was definitely teamwork-challenged and probably drove the trainers into another line of work. What was supposed to teach us that we needed each other only brought our personal junk out in the open for all to see.

The athletic adventurous types in the group, with their abundance of hubris, found new and innovative ways to prove that "I'm better than you are" while still looking like team players. At the other end of the spectrum, one woman who'd had a terrible accident on the high ropes in a high school gym class couldn't bring herself to do the rope ladder walk. Bypassing the high-wire act, she felt she had let down the team and lost ground with her peers by exposing her vulnerability. I know. I was that woman.

I strongly advocate cooperation and teamwork. Who doesn't prefer a peer environment to a rigid hierarchical model? But the kind of community that satisfies our deepest longing to be known by others will not be found at work. God intended His family here on earth to be our frontline community.

Say what? Do you feel like God needs a reminder about the Christians who have hurt you over the years when you gave community a whirl?

Admittedly, church can be as unsafe as the workplace. Insecure jockeying for position, personal agendas and the ability to inflict pain do not mysteriously leave our nature when the Holy Spirit takes up residence. We are personally under renovation by the Holy Spirit until we reach heaven's front porch. But God does not excuse us from spiritual community because it's tough. He considers it a valuable perk of our adoption into the family of faith.

Romans 12:10-21 serves up a generous description of what spiritual community is supposed to look like. "Be devoted to one another. . . . Honor one another above yourselves. . . . Share with God's people who are in need. Practice hospitality. . . . Live in harmony. . . . Do not be proud, but be willing to associate with people of low position. Do not be conceited. Do not repay anyone evil for evil. . . . As far as it depends on you, live at peace with everyone." The church is *supposed* to be the place where it's safe to be ourselves.

How is authentic community possible in light of our sinful nature? Larry Crabb, in his book *The Safest Place on Earth*, says it takes admitting daily our brokenness and acknowledging our desperate dependence on the Holy Spirit to show us how to get it right.

"Everything in spiritual community is reversed from the world's order," Crabb writes. "It is our weakness, not our competence, that moves others; our sorrows, not our blessings, that break down the barriers of fear and shame that keep us apart; our admitted failures, not our paraded successes, that bind us together in hope."[2]

How ironic! If one of us takes off our mask, exposes our vulnerability and lays down judgments and power struggles, then others may feel safe doing the same. How unlike the workplace, where appearances are everything and any admitted weakness is seized upon and used to another's advantage.

The trick is that somebody has to blink first and take the risk. This is one time where you get no points for deferring. ("You go first. No, you go first. No, I insist, you go first.") We are invited by God to engage in spiritual community as if we truly belong—because we do.

Choose to be a player. Help create a winsome brand of genuine spiritual community that will leave workplace community in the dust.

Reality

- [ ] Have you subconsciously made a judgment that it's not really possible in this day and age to live out the kind of community described in Romans 12?

- [ ] What past wounds have fostered that attitude, and what are you prepared to do about them?

- [ ] Who are the people in your current circle of friends with whom you can begin to take steps toward building deeper community?

Whatever Happened to Green Pastures and Still Waters?

If you were to draw a picture of contentment, what would it look like? What images are big enough to represent your view of utter satisfaction? Would it be you and your family gathered in the backyard on a Sunday afternoon, the sun shining, one of you hovering over the grill, the kids playing together without fighting, everyone healthy and the bills paid? Would you be satisfied just to *have* a family instead of being alone? Maybe it's a picture of you with the young child you're mentoring, huddled over schoolbooks in an inner-city church basement, knowing you're making a difference in another person's life.

Several years ago, a man said to me, "When I see you conclude a project or reach a milestone, you check it off your 'To Do' list and move on, like you're playing 'Beat the Clock.' Do you ever sit back and savor anything? You act like all your Kodak moments are for someone else to en-joy."

His observation came as a total surprise. It wasn't a conscious thing. I was too focused on being in the game to notice. There would be time to savor . . . later.

The point is, whatever I was striving for was out there somewhere in the distance, just outside my grasp. I wasn't sure exactly what contentment looked like, but it wasn't here . . . now.

In her book *Downshifting: Reinventing Success on a Slower Track*, business journalist and editor Amy Saltzman de-scribes frequent walks down Newark Street, a prestigious address on the northwest side of Washington, D.C.

The immaculately restored million-dollar Victorian homes feature romantic wrap-around front porches with wicker furniture, rag rugs and porch boxes of flowers. It's a place where you expect to see people curled up with a book, without a care in the world, sipping fresh-brewed iced tea.

Saltzman says it dawned on her one day that in all the times she had walked along Newark Street she never saw anyone sitting on those porches. The people who lived there apparently purchased their image of contentment but didn't have the life.[1]

The fallacy lies in thinking contentment is a by-product of something we acquire or a reward we gain for something we accomplish. "When my business finally turns a profit, then I'll feel some peace." "When my kids have graduated from college, then I'll be happy." "When I get thin thighs, then I'll be content with my body" (which, in my case, will happen right after pigs fly). When *this* happens . . . when *that's* done. . . . Quick, grab your camera. We have a lot of pictures to take. When will it be enough?

Nelson Rockefeller, one of the wealthiest men of his time, was once asked, "What will it take to make you happy?" He reportedly replied, "A little bit more."

In the Old Testament, David, a former shepherd, paints a different picture of contentment in the 23rd Psalm. His idea of the good life is not a cruise in the Mediterranean without those stupid, smelly sheep. He doesn't wistfully yearn for an ivory-handled rosewood Power Shepherd's Staff with a built-in Swiss Army knife.

For his picture of peace, David looks with new eyes at a familiar scene. He draws from his old job as shepherd. His old workplace, the harsh, unforgiving terrain of rural Israel, was a tough place to find contentment. There was constant threat of attack by predators and struggles with drought and starvation. The sheep were dumb as a box of rocks and continually wandered off. Yet, in David's view, if peace was worth having, it had to be possible in the midst of familiar, tedious, exhausting real life. If it took special circumstances or accessories, there would always be the chance it could be taken away.

David pictures his old stomping ground from God's point of view, and everything looks different. You can almost feel him exhale with relief.

- "The LORD is my shepherd, I shall not be in want" (23:1). This pasture, where God's in charge, is lush, with plenty of water nearby, assuring that neither He nor His flock will starve. *His needs will be met.*

- "He makes me lie down in green pastures, he leads me beside quiet waters, he restores my soul" (23:2-3). David can relax because a Chief Shepherd more competent than him now manages Shepherd World. *Everything is under control.*

- "He guides me in paths of righteousness for his name's sake" (23:3). David doesn't have to figure things out on his own. *He will be taught how to live.*

- "Even though I walk through the valley of the shadow of death, I will fear no evil, for you are with me; your rod and your staff, they comfort me"(23:4). He's safe, protected and supported. *There's nothing to fear.*

It makes you want to sign up for Shepherd School.

I like this new brand of contentment. It stands up to all kinds of conditions. It's not dependent on me becoming senior vice president of West Pasture or having the largest wool output in the last decade or the biggest herd. It's portable. If I lose my job, I don't have to leave contentment behind. No batteries required. Anyone can have it. And it's possible right now. It's a keeper.

I'm comforted by Paul's words in Philippians 4:11-12 that this kind of contentment isn't a perspective that comes naturally—at least not at first. He said it had to be nurtured. ". . . for I have *learned* the secret of being content in any and every situation" (4:11, author's paraphrase, emphasis added).

I'm working on it. I've learned that contentment isn't about getting what you want. It's about wanting what you have and believing it's enough.

My pasture is starting to look pretty good.

Reality

☐ What is your picture of contentment?

☐ Has it changed in the last five, ten or twenty years?

☐ Do you currently consider yourself a contented person?

☐ What do you savor about your life right now?

☐ What circumstances pose a special challenge to contentment? Talk to God about it.

What Are We Here to Do?

Companies going through organizational change often adopt a management process or system to give structure and language to what is happening. They bear names like Management of Change, Continuous Quality Improvement (CQI) and Total Quality Management (TQM). It's a way of saying, "We're not going to do things the way we've always done them." An important part of these systems is changing *how* decisions are made as well as changing the decisions themselves.

Most of us don't give much thought to how we make decisions. It's one of those basic life skills we pick up along the way and use dozens of times a day with mixed results, hoping to get better at it as we mature.

We know good decisions make a difference in how well our lives turn out. And since God cares how our lives turn out, it's safe to assume He's interested in how we make decisions. Beyond that, the specifics of His involvement are less clear. It basically means we ask for His input and try to align our decisions with His values, right?

Yes. But what if how we make decisions inadvertently sabotages our ability to know God's mind on a matter? What if we're working with a faulty decision-making process?

Think about how you make decisions. It's probably some variation of the following:

- Know clearly what you must decide.

- Identify your ultimate objective.

- Get good advice.

- Weigh the options.

- Play out the consequences and trade-offs.

- Pray.

- Decide.

Sounds pretty basic: Have a plan. Work the plan. Ask God to guide you. See where the information leads. The Bible applauds this kind of careful deliberating. "Be sure you have sound advice before making plans" (Proverbs 20:18, CEV). "God's people think before they take a step" (21:29, CEV). So far, so good.

But what about all the unconscious attitudes, expectations and assumptions we bring to the table when we make a decision? When and where are they factored in?

Management consultants know that those unspoken beliefs and perceptions buried deep in a company's culture play a major role in what decisions get made and an organization's subsequent ability to adapt to change or move in another direction.

If it's true for companies, it's even truer for individuals. Our deeply rooted attitudes, expectations and assumptions are like the 8,000-pound gorilla in the room when we make a decision. We can pretend it's not there or not important, but every time we make a move, we bump into it. It's stupid to ignore it.

What if God wanted to take you somewhere different in your career or your marriage or your life in general? Could He get through the layers of "anything but," "not now," "only if" and "yeah, but" and reach your heart with His plan? Those kind of words are a tip-off that there are gorillas in the room.

Failure to acknowledge their influence means we're skewing the outcome. Our decisions will be fairly predictable and probably won't rock any boats. Sadly, they also may have nothing to do with what God wants. God often wants us out of the boat or, at the very least, untethered from the dock and moving into deeper waters. How is He going to get us out there if our decision-making process doesn't allow for it?

Being openhearted to God means laying down any attitudes that obstruct His "moving around" room. God is not free to guide us fully to the best decision until we give up instructing Him what our life has to look like in order for us to be happy. He knows what will make us happy. He's God!

Since most of us have strong defense mechanisms that kick in whenever the status quo is challenged, we may need help naming our gorillas.

The Quakers use a process called "clearness committees." The person asking for help lays out his or her dilemma—a job offer, a move, a relationship or whatever. One by one, those who participate ask the person questions, listen intently, reflect back what they hear and make personal observations. A recording clerk notes unifying threads that emerge.

Sometimes there are long periods of silence between comments. Quakers say the silence gives individuals time to lay down their personal opinions and natural human tendency to "fix" the other person. It makes room for a collective sense of God's underlying truth to emerge. The eventual solution or course of action may be far different than anything anyone envisioned at the beginning.

Some would say these groups are doing nothing more than exercising the spiritual gift of discernment. But they are also stepping aside, giving up their own biases so God can really direct and influence the outcome. And the person seeking help is allowing his or her gorillas to be exposed in the process. In the end, God has a voice not only in what is decided but also in how the decision is made.

I sat in a meeting once with a group of Christian leaders trying to determine the direction of a ministry. There was a lot of talking going on but not much listening. The participants seemed primarily interested in winning each other over to their particular point of view. Late in the meeting, a wise older gentlemen entered the room to join us. Everyone rushed to fill him in on the various options on the table. He listened patiently, then said simply, "Has the Holy Spirit showed up yet?"

Until God is in the house, decision-making is little more than a group grope for wisdom. If I want my decisions to be as full of God as possible, I need to make room for Him. My 8,000-pound gorillas will have to wait outside.

Reality

☐ How do you make decisions?

☐ Is there room in your decision-making process for God to intervene with a challenge or direction that's outside your comfort level?

☐ Name your biggest gorilla. Can you think of a recent decision that was unduly influenced by unconscious biases or perceptions? Did it have a good effect or bad effect on the outcome?

☐ Talk to God about how you make decisions and how you want to change the process.

In Praise of Praise

here were you July 20, 1969? *Apollo 11* astronaut Buzz Aldrin was taking communion—on the moon. During the radio blackout immediately after the Eagle lunar module landed, Aldrin pulled out of his flight gear a small communion cup, given to him by his church, and two tiny plastic packages filled with communion elements. He set them down on the small table in front of the abort-guidance computer, alongside a Scripture reading he brought along for the occasion. Then he announced to Mission Control that man had, indeed, finally made it to the moon.

"Houston, this is LM Pilot speaking. I would like to request a few moments of silence," Aldrin told Mission Control. "I would like to invite each person listening in, wherever and whomever he may be, to contemplate for a moment the events of the past few hours and give thanks in his own individual way."

Aldrin wanted to read the Scripture passage that lay in front of him, but NASA had nixed the idea. The space agency was already knee-deep in a court battle with religious opponent Madelyn Murray O'Hare because the *Apollo 8* crew read from Genesis while orbiting the moon at Christmas.

During the moment of silence, Aldrin took communion as he read John 15:5 to himself. "I am the vine; you are the branches. If a man remains in me and I in him, he will bear much fruit; apart from me you can do nothing." He agreed with God and gave thanks.[1]

I'm glad Buzz Aldrin knew who to thank. I suspect, however, that hurtling through the galaxy like a speck of dust would make a true believer out of anyone. In some ways, I think it's tougher for those of us who are earth-bound to know our place in the universe.

Sure, we understand God deserves credit for creating the cosmos. And there's no disputing the glorious gift of our salvation that was all His doing, aided by His precious son, Jesus. It's also not a stretch to thank God for the gifts and talents He deposited in us at birth.

It's the part *after* that that occasionally blurs. We act like God dropped our talents at the door and hurried off, and everything we've accomplished since then has been the result of our own hard work and sacrifice. "He got the ball rolling, but look at what I've done with it! I ought to get a bonus." Self-sufficiency, by definition, limits gratitude.

Then there's the fact that expressing thanks is the thing "nice" people do in our culture. You don't have to be religious. We teach children to say "please" and "thank you" from the time they can talk. Young couples spend the first year of their marriage penning formal notes of appreciation to people they haven't seen in years. It's part of the social contract between civilized people.

Add it all up, and our thanks to God can look more like a magnanimous gesture of thoughtfulness on our part—because we're nice people. "Let's give the Creator a nice round of applause for His contribution. Nice job, God. We're glad You're on our team."

Wrong answer.

Expressing true spiritual gratitude to God is as much for our sake as His. It alters our internal compass. We realize we're part of the grand scheme of things, but we're not the axis. It helps us get over ourselves and get over the delusion of self-sufficiency. It aligns us to the truth about how things really are.

God's been warning His children for centuries that this could be a problem. It happened to the children of Israel in the desert. You'd think after being led out of Egypt with only the clothes on their back—totally de-pendent on God for food, clothes and shelter for forty years—that it wouldn't be an issue. But Moses had to spell it out for them again in Deuteronomy 8.

He said when they arrived in the Promised Land and settled down in cities they didn't build, with wells they didn't dig and vineyards they didn't plant, they should be careful to acknowledge who made it all possible.

> Otherwise, when you eat and are satisfied, when you build fine houses and settle down, and when your herds and flocks grow large and your silver and

gold increase and all you have is multiplied, then your heart will become proud and you will forget the LORD your God. . . . *He* led you through the vast and dreadful desert. . . . *He* brought you water out of hard rock. *He* gave you manna to eat. . . . You may say to yourself, "My power and the strength of my hands have produced this wealth for me." But *remember* the LORD your God, for it is *he* who gives you the ability to produce wealth. . . ." (8:12-18, emphasis added)

None of this has to do with net worth. It's about understanding our position. We are blessed because He chose to bless us, regardless of our station in life. He invites us to come along for the ride, specks of dust that we are.

Hey, you with the full cup—lavish praise on Him! There's more where that came from.

Reality

- [ ] Has your gratitude been limited by self-sufficiency?

- [ ] What are you most grateful for today?

- [ ] Are there things for which you've failed to give God credit?

- [ ] Do you tend to focus on your lack rather than what you have?

- [ ] Keep a small notebook or pad beside your bed at night, and before you go to sleep, write down a sign of God's blessing on you that day. When you get discouraged, pull our your Blessings Book and remember.

Secrets from the Underground

There's nothing good to be said about holding on to something dead. When objects at the back of my refrigerator start to resemble alien life forms, I want them outta there. As an avid gardener, I know that dead branches and stems on shrubs and flowers are not healthy and hurt the plant's long-term prospects. Growth is stunted. Flowers stop blooming. Sucker growths pop up and sap valuable life from a plant's main stem. I want flowers, not wild, mangy foliage, so I prune with a vengeance.

When I read John 15:2 where Jesus uses a pruning metaphor to talk about how God—like a gardner—increases our fruitfulness, I'm with Him all the way. It makes perfect sense when Jesus says, "He cuts off every branch in me that bears no fruit, while every branch that does bear fruit he prunes so that it will be even more fruitful."

What's not to like about getting rid of whatever makes me less effective—that sucker growth that hinders me from blossoming into all God intended? "Have at it, God." It's like getting a good haircut to eliminate the split ends, right?

But then there's that other metaphor Jesus uses when He talks about bearing fruit. "I tell you the truth, unless a kernel of wheat falls to the ground and dies, it remains only a single seed. But if it dies, it produces many seeds" (12:24).

"Uh, dying? Hey, I want to be as fruitful as the next person, but dying? That wasn't exactly what I had in mind, God. It's terribly . . . well, you know . . . inconvenient. I don't get to pack a suitcase of my favorite things. There's no going back. I'm not in charge anymore. Isn't there some other way we can do this?"

Refusal to let God do whatever is necessary, or attempts to prune ourselves so God won't have to do it, are just excuses to take God's job away from Him and stay in control. We're not nearly as good at this as He is. Besides, we don't have the guts to go as deep as may be necessary, and we are unlikely to orchestrate our own dying. Self-preservation kicks in, and we stop short.

We don't get it. Dying is good for us. The death of all that's not under God's authority is necessary to make room for what He has waiting in the wings. The old and new don't successfully cohabit over the long haul. Those pitiful decaying parts of us from our past—the ones we drag around like dead limbs—rot whatever they touch, but it's still hard for us to let go of what's familiar.

God, on the other hand, is fearless. He doesn't hesitate to act when drastic measures are appropriate, because He sees the outcome up ahead.

I was once operated on for a surface-spreading melanoma. It showed up out of the blue and was growing fast. Surgery was scheduled immediately.

The surgeon, in explaining the skin graft surgery he was about to perform, said, "I'm not sure how deep I'll have to go to get it all. It may require severing your ankle tendon, in which case you won't be able to flex your foot again. But if we don't get all the cancer, you still may not be able to flex your foot again because the cancer could take your life. So I'm going to go as deep as I have to go to get the best outcome."

That was many years ago, and I've been cancer-free since. I'm glad he was ruthless in attacking the cancer.

For some reason, though, when God works on our hearts and minds to perform deep surgery, I don't understand as clearly that it's a matter of life and death. I find it hard to be grateful that God is going as deep as He has to go to get the best outcome.

Once, during a particularly painful season when God was putting to death whole chunks of my life, I complained to a friend that God's tactics were "killing me."

"That's wonderful!" he said.

"And this would be . . . uh . . . comforting?" I said sarcastically.

"Sounds like God brought out the Deep Ripper." The Deep Ripper, he explained, is a farm implement that looks like a medieval torture device. It restores a dead or barren field to productivity. The field may look fine on the surface—which is why no one sees there's a problem until one day the field is simply not productive anymore.

On closer inspection, the farmer discovers that a "hard pan" of rock-solid earth has formed six to twelve inches underground. It's a natural consequence, he said, of years of hardships the land endures—storms, drought and other beatings. Eventually, its life is sucked dry.

Some of us have an imperceptible layer of hard pan in our hearts from enduring years of unrelenting stress and the surprises life randomly dispenses. It shouldn't surprise us if one day we come up empty.

New growth can't penetrate the hard pan, my friend told me. Cultivating, fertilizing and the usual restorative procedures are useless. It takes the Deep Ripper with its three-foot-long spikes to shake things up.

"Yes," I sighed. "That's what it feels like."

"Well, here's the good part," he said. "The process can feel pretty violent at the time, but eventually the field is more productive than ever. Hang on. The best is yet to come."

That sounds like Jesus. He's no more fond of dead things than I am. Every time He talked about death, it was usually a warm-up for what He really loved to talk about—new life. In fact, He taught us, by example, the central truth about new life. There can be no Easter without Good Friday first.

Reality

☐ In what areas of your life have you resisted God's pruning? Is it a control issue?

☐ Has a hard pan developed in your heart?

☐ Do you believe God is better at pruning away the dead parts of your life that you are?

☐ Tell Him how far you are willing to let Him go in your life to make you more fruitful.

You CAN Get There from Here

esus and I have very different ideas about life direction. I want to know where I'm going, how long it will take to get there, what I should take with me, how long I'll be gone and what to expect along the way.

Jesus says, "Follow Me." Period. No maps. No estimated time of arrival. There's not even a marker that says, "You are here."

I once heard about a cloister monk who spent forty-eight hours with Mother Theresa observing her ministry on the streets of Calcutta. At the end of his visit, he asked Mother Theresa to pray for him that God would give him direction about the future course of his life.

"I refuse," she reportedly answered. "God didn't promise us clarity. He promised to be with us until the end and to get us to where we need to be. I will pray instead that you will know God can be trusted for the journey."

The Bible is crammed with people who decided to follow God without knowing exactly where they were going. I read their stories, mystified by their ability to lay aside their questions.

In Genesis 12, God told Abram to leave his country and his people so God could take him to a destination to be named later. The only information Abram was given was details about the reward he would enjoy for following God's instruction.

"I will make you into a great nation," God said, "and I will bless you. . . . All peoples on earth will be blessed through you" (12:2-3). It was an extraordinary promise. Then again, from my vantage point, it was pretty nonspecific. Like the used car salesman who says, "This beauty is still good for a lot of miles." Define "a lot."

I think God expected a lot from Abraham—a lot more than I could have delivered under the same circumstances.

If someone told you he had a job opportunity for you in another city—job description, living arrangements, salary and location unknown—and if he said you needed to sell your house, leave your friends and church and relatives and hit the road, would you do it? Especially if the person said, "The details? Oh, they come later."

I don't think so.

Incredibly, though, Genesis 12:4 says, "Abram left, as the LORD had told him." Just like that. God says leave. Abram starts packing. How did he do that?

The clues are in Abraham's story. He spent enough time intimately relating to God to realize God knew what He was doing. He remembered all the times God had come through for him in the past. He didn't know the plan, but he trusted the Person in charge of the plan. His life was safer with God than any of the alternatives.

If I spent enough time with God, praying and listening and reading His Word to know what He's like and how He operates, I might not need to pester Him for details about what's coming. I would know that He has promised to hear my voice above all the rest when I cry out to Him. There would be no doubt in my mind that the unfinished business of my life has His undivided attention.

If I spent enough time with God, so the Holy Spirit could bring to mind other times when I didn't know where I was going or how to get there and somehow I made it, I would recall that the path was not a straight line and may have included a few ditches—but He never abandoned me.

I think it offends God when we tell Him how to do His job or when we act like He can't devise a plan for us that we'll like—without our help. It's like telling God, "You can send me anywhere as long as the year-round temperature is between 60 and 80 degrees, I have a wood-burning fireplace in my home, flowers in my backyard and a Starbucks coffee shop within five minutes of my house." Besides, it's exhausting to play God when you're not God.

I think it's equally offensive to God—maybe more so—to tell God all the reasons His plans won't work. "God, what were You thinking? You know I don't have the patience to do this. I can't afford the pay cut. It's outside my skill set. You want me to be happy, don't You? Then You can't be serious about wanting me to do *this*."

Job wrestled with this. "God, what on earth are You doing? What's going on?" his words imply. I'm intrigued that God never answered Job's question directly. However, in Job 38-41, God reminded him who he was dealing with.

"Job, did *you* mark off the dimensions of the earth? Do *you* tell the sea's waves to go this far and no further? Do lightning bolts report to *you*? Have *you* ever told the dawn its place?"

Job, appropriately stunned, replies in Job 42:2, "I know that you can do all things; no plan of yours can be thwarted."

That's the bottom line. It's not about getting answers, but it is about understanding Who we are dealing with and sticking close to the One who has the answers.

He may keep us on a "need to know" basis, but, if we get with the program, we'll make it to our destination.

Reality

☐ What areas of your life would especially benefit right now from clearer guidance?

☐ Are you finding it particularly hard to trust that God has a plan?

☐ What do you clearly understand about how He guides?

☐ What part is difficult to handle?

☐ Think about how far you've come and what it took to get here. What part did God play? Have you thanked Him?

☐ Talk to Him about where you're struggling in the area of accepting His guidance.

Do You Suppose God Grades on a Curve?

J wasn't feeling well the day it happened. I had been working in my home office all morning, battling a splitting headache and fatigue. Finally, after lunch, I lay down for a nap—something I never do. I thought maybe I'd picked up a virus.

Because of street noise outside my window, I put in earplugs so I could rest undisturbed. I fell into a deep sleep, sleeping much longer than planned.

A few hours later, shaking off the grogginess, I got up and walked down the hall to my office to get back to work. Everything but the furniture was gone. Phones, fax machine, computer and printer, books, files, office supplies—gone. No Post-it notes or appointment book. The loose-leaf notebook with the working draft of this book was not there. File cabinets were pulled open and empty. The whimsical mementos that litter my desk and sideboard had vanished.

I could barely breathe. My heart pounded like a jackhammer. *I've been robbed! Why would anyone want my files? How did they get into the house without me hearing them?* I whirled around and raced downstairs to check the rest of the house.

Everything was untouched, right down to the unread mail on the dining room table. *What's happening? Am I losing my mind?* I sprinted back upstairs to confirm what I had seen. Standing in the doorway to my office, I started to cry. It was as if a huge part of me didn't exist anymore. There was nothing to verify I was a consultant or journalist or a speaker. There were no dog-eared books to give clues to what I'm passionate about. My nature photography had been unceremoniously stripped from the walls.

Then it was over. I woke up . . . *really* woke up. It had been a dream. A dream within a dream.

Do you feel tricked? Or are you thinking, "She must be pretty stupid to think I'd fall for something that lame." Either way, I may have created a credibility gap that, without a reasonable explanation, could jeopardize your future interest in anything I have to say.

That's exactly what happens in a life without integrity. Our words and our actions don't tell the same story. We can carry it off for awhile, but eventually people sense something doesn't add up.

Proverbs 10:9 says, "The man of integrity walks securely, but he who takes crooked paths will be found out."

There's a steadiness that comes when our inner values line up with our outward behavior. You don't have to worry about keeping your stories straight. There's only one story.

Explaining becomes an added tool for understanding rather than a curtain to hide what's behind Door #2.

One of Satan's most effective weapons for diluting the spiritual potency of men and women of faith is to undermine their congruence. Like a downhill stream that always finds a way around obstacles in its path, we can expect Satan to press and prod and poke continually, looking for that point of vulnerability in our commitment to Christ. His goal is to throw us off balance and destroy our credibility . . . bit by bit by bit. From his point of view, the steadiness that comes from integrity has got to go.

When we talk of making faith an integral part of our lives, we usually mean that faith should be interrelated to all of life. *Integral* comes from the same root word as *integrity*. When faith is interrelated to all of life, we have integrity—soundness of mind, body and spirit.

I have a pendulum clock that sits on my mantle. The pendulum sways in steady syncopation day in and day out, without variation. You can look at it any hour of the night or day, and nothing about the clock changes except the hands that move in response to the energy provided by the pendulum. The pendulum acts the same way wherever it is placed. Climate and circumstances and whoever is in proximity to it don't affect it. The only thing that can stop it is the absence of its energy source—a battery. If the battery is old or dead or missing, the pendulum grinds to a halt.

We can't live a life of integrity based on an old, tired or dead faith. Our batteries run down. After a while, instead of consistently making choices that are beyond reproach, we lose our resolve. The danger of spiritual deadness looms. The lines get blurred. We get confused about what's right and what's not. We get tired and don't feel like being a person of integrity.

God's not surprised. He never intended for us to muster integrity on our own. He expects us to return to Him again and again for recharging. Philippians 4:13 says, "I can do everything through him who gives me strength." Present tense.

Today, right now, you can stop what you're doing and connect with your heavenly Power Source. You can pick up your Bible, pray, pop a worship CD in your player or sit quietly and listen for the leadings of the Holy Spirit. You can find out what Jesus would do.

Best of all, you won't wake up and find it's all a dream.

Reality

- [ ] Name one person you know who immediately comes to mind as a person of integrity. What is it about him that convinces you?

- [ ] Would people who know you consider you a person of integrity?

- [ ] What are your areas of vulnerability? Are they related to how fresh your walk with God is?

- [ ] Tell God what you need from Him right now.

The Art of Shutting Up

I met Yvette on a ministry trip to Belfast, Northern Ireland. I was part of a support team participating in a conference on evangelism and reconciliation. From the moment we landed, the Irish were so warm and hospitable that it was hard to believe we were in a country plagued by a centuries-old bloody conflict.

We stayed in a hotel surrounded by twelve-foot-high barbed wire fences and a constant military patrol. When we checked in, the desk clerk said in a cheery, lilting brogue, "Welcome to our reopening! Doesn't everything look lovely?" Then she leaned over and in a conspiratorial whisper added, "It's actually our twenty-second reopening. We've had a wee bit of a bombing problem, you know." Uhhh . . . right. A wee bit.

As the conference got underway, I wondered what it would take to communicate God's love at this time, in this place, to these people? During the music part of the

213

worship service, I stopped singing and found myself using American Sign Language instead. I'm not very good at it, but I fall back on it when words don't seem enough.

After the service, a Presbyterian minister approached me. He led a small church for the deaf. He'd seen me signing and asked if I'd be willing to meet Yvette.

The teenager was not deaf, but she had asked him to teach her sign language so she wouldn't have to speak. I was intrigued, and we arranged a meeting.

Yvette was a beautiful brunette with a porcelain complexion and riveting eyes. At age three, she saw her father beat her mother so severely it drove her mother insane. She never saw her mother again. Traumatized, Yvette lost her ability to talk normally. Her face, neck and throat muscles violently contorted each time she tried to speak. It was painful to watch.

I traffic in words—spoken and written. They're my link to everyone and everything. But the last thing this tormented young woman needed was my words. She needed to be heard.

Quietly, I laid my hand on hers and told her I would listen to everything she wanted to tell me for as long as it took. And it took a long time because communication was so difficult.

Laboriously she explained how she'd been shuffled from relative to relative, each of them doling out relentless ridicule and humiliation. Her disability shamed the family, she was told. Finally, one day she left home for good.

She described the day she stopped feeling anymore and talked about her disappointment with God, whom she had asked to heal her every day since her mother disappeared.

As she spoke, I silently asked the Holy Spirit what would help her in that moment. I had a dozen follow-up questions I wanted to ask. I had important observations to make (or so I thought), Scripture to share about God's love in adversity and a compelling action plan. But as I heard her story—too moved to utter any well-intentioned words—I realized, quite accidentally, that sometimes love just listens.

Listening is a powerful form of communication. It's the aggressive humble pursuit of what's on the heart and mind of someone else—a deliberate effort to respect and understand the other person's point of view. It's not natural. It's not passive. It's both a skill and a responsibility. It's definitely not something I do well, as my friends will attest.

The trap for capable, hard-charging Christians—especially those with leadership gifts—is that they always have something to say. Whether it's on the job or in a ministry setting, their words probably *are* worth hearing.

But sometimes love listens.

James 1:19 says, "My dear brothers, take note of this: Everyone should be quick to listen, slow to speak and slow to become angry." Sheila Walsh calls it the ministry of presence, of being there and paying attention.

I met with Yvette several times over the next three days. I consider it one of the more important things I've ever done. Before I left Ireland, she asked me to pray with her and to suggest a Bible verse she could think about on her journey back to God.

I suggested Psalm 27:13-14. "I am still confident of this: I will see the goodness of the LORD in the land of the living. Wait for the LORD; be strong and take heart and wait for the LORD."

Because God *is* listening.

☐ How well do you listen?

☐ How would the important relationships of your life benefit from you becoming a more active listener?

☐ Are there certain people you especially have trouble listening to? Why?

☐ Do *you* feel heard?

☐ Are there things you've needed to talk about, and there was no one to listen?

☐ Ask God to connect you with a trusted confidante and for the courage to share your story.

Sometimes You Need a Dog

My dog Tillie idolizes me. I like that in a dog. I do wish she'd be a little less expressive when I first walk in the door and she body slams into me with her 100-pound hunk of burning love. Overall, though, her unabashed devotion works wonders on my spirit after a bad day.

Loyalty—whether to one person or to an organization or belief system—is not highly valued or expected anymore in the marketplace. Roger Rosenblatt, one of America's premier essayists, noted the trend in an article he amusingly titled, "Stand by Me—for a Moment." Human beings are fickle by nature, and it seems to be getting worse.

During my years with an international public relations agency, I worked with several Fortune 500 consumer product companies. Our account teams helped them introduce new products like Kraft fat-free salad dressings and Degree deodorant. There was always talk about building "brand loyalty" to keep customers coming back.

Loyalty never seemed like the right word since any allegiance was clearly based on both sides getting something. You take care of me (give me the kind of product I want) and I'll take care of you (and keep buying your product). Any so-called loyalty would disappear overnight if either side failed to uphold its end of the transaction.

I received a painful personal taste of transactional loyalty several years ago when I went to work for a Chicago radio station which had been recently purchased by Mutual Broadcasting. Mutual converted the station to a news-talk format with the goal of toppling the long-time king of Chicago newsradio, WBBM-AM, the local CBS news giant.

Media observers thought Mutual was nuts to take on the challenge, but we didn't care. The newly assembled team felt like we were on a mission together. It energized our uphill efforts.

I was a general assignment reporter covering news stories out in the field. The stars of the station were the talk show hosts back in the studio who held court several hours a day juggling live interviews, listener call-ins, news, traffic, weather and the rest.

One morning, I stopped by the newsroom on my way to a 10 a.m. press conference. As I walked in, the midmorning talk show host and her producer were walking out—as in *walking out* over a contract dispute or some other precipitating event. None of us was quite sure what happened, but we knew it was forty minutes until airtime, and there was no "B" team on hand to host the show.

Most stations have carefully laid contingency plans and backup hosts three deep to protect themselves in such a situation. The station, however, had a new team on board and apparently didn't have plans in place yet. The news director turned to me and said, "OK, you're our morning host. Do whatever you need to do to get ready."

No guests were booked (a tactical ploy by the departing team) and, at that point in my career, I'd never done a live talk show—only prerecorded ones. At most 50,000-watt stations in a major market, in a pinch you can open the phone lines and let callers drive the discussion. Unfortunately, our still-new format had a listening audience of about four people, three of whom had already called in that morning.

In desperation, I talked that morning about anything I could think of. Everything I ever learned, heard someone else say or ever thought about saying became fodder for on-air discussion. My friends say I haven't stopped talking since! I blame it all on that morning when I learned about loyalty.

It's not loyalty unless it's there when the chips are down—when it costs to stand and deliver. We find out how much something is worth to us when the price goes up.

It got me thinking about how loyal I am to God and to my beliefs when I'm out in the thick of it in the work world. Would people with whom I cross professional paths be surprised to learn I'm a Christian? Or, at the other end of the spectrum, if I'm explicit about my faith, does my behavior reinforce my spiritual claims or make a mockery of them?

I suspect that's why Peter's triple denial must have been so painful to Jesus. Peter was the first disciple called to follow Jesus. He was in Jesus' inner circle and often acted as spokesman for the disciples. He was one of the few invited to witness Jesus' transfiguration and the raising of Jairus' daughter from the dead. Jesus asked Peter to come along for moral support when He went to Gethsemane to pray the night before His crucifixion. Only John had a closer relationship to Jesus.

In short, Jesus trusted Peter. He gave the impetuous disciple every advantage, despite Peter's histrionics. But Peter blew it with denials that were as grandiose as his devotion. When the price for loyalty to Jesus went up, Peter apparently didn't have enough faith in his account to cover it—at least not yet.

I wince when I read those denials. It hits too close to home. I haven't gone around openly disavowing allegiance to Jesus, but then, I also haven't seen Jesus—the person in whom I've banked my future—led away by soldiers for execution. Even without those stakes, I can point to plenty of times when my inaction or decidedly unChristlike behavior indicts me. And I haven't always acted like someone whom Jesus trusted and loved and gave the advantage of forgiveness and eternal life.

Sheila Walsh asks, "How would you feel if a movie was made of your life and nothing was left out? The good news is that God has seen your movie and loves you anyway." How does He do it?

"Great is his love toward us, and the faithfulness of the LORD endures forever," the psalmist says (Psalm 117:2). God doesn't give up on us just as He didn't give up on Peter. In fact, He wrote the book on loyalty—and paid a very high price to prove it.

Reality

- [ ] Have you been loyal to Christ, or are there areas in which you deny Him?

- [ ] What could you do to demonstrate your loyalty more faithfully?

- [ ] What makes loyalty difficult in certain situations?

- [ ] What is it likely to cost you?

- [ ] Are you ready to pay the price?

"Let's Do Lunch. . . . Have Your People Call My People"

Corporate America loves consultants, the business professionals paid extraordinary fees to tell companies what they often can't hear from an insider.

It's an unwritten axiom of business that if you have an unpopular initiative to promote or a problem you can't solve without considerable fallout, your best bet is to hire a consultant to deliver the bad news.

We are equally awash in experts on a personal level. We turn to psychotherapists, nutrition counselors, personal trainers, fashion consultants, interior design consultants, financial planners and success coaches to tell us what we need—what will make us happy and solve our problems. The beauty of these on-call gurus is that we can listen to their advice and reject what we don't like. *We* remain solidly at the helm.

For years, I treated God as my chief spiritual consultant. I asked His advice about jobs, relationships, ministry opportunities, money management and future direction. I pressed Him for speedy answers to urgent problems. I carefully instructed Him on what I required for true happiness. I even gave Him deadlines by which time I needed answers.

When I got answers I liked, my praise and gratitude followed. When the silence was deafening or when the Holy Spirit pierced my heart about an attitude or an unconfessed sin or pocket of stubbornness, I negotiated. Surely God misunderstood what I meant.

At some point in the learning curve of what it means to be in relationship with Him, the obvious began to dawn: God thought He had the right to meddle in any corner of my life that needed it. Imagine that! Who did He think He was? God?

In the children's classic, *The Lion, the Witch and the Wardrobe*, C.S. Lewis makes it clear that God is not tame. He just won't "settle down." One of the children in the story asks whether Aslan, the Lion who represents Christ, is safe. "Who said anything about safe?" comes the reply. " 'Course he isn't safe. But he's good. He's the King, I tell you."[1]

God is not satisfied to serve as a benign spiritual consultant. He's Demolition Man when it comes to going after what has junked up our lives. Can you blame Him? He put a lot on the line for our relationship.

He also knows that left to our own devices we will follow the path of least resistance as Eve demonstrated so effectively in the Garden of Eden.

A dear friend of mine, who was not a Christian at the time, said to me once, "So you really believe all that business about us being sinners at heart? Well, you're wrong. I know lots of people who are loving and moral who don't believe in God. You just have to decide what kind of person you want to be, and your behavior will follow."

"Really?" I said. "Have you ever watched two-year-olds play with each other unsupervised? Within ten minutes, they're ready to kill each other because one of them can't get his or her way. The only difference between them and adults is that we learn how to wrap our willfulness in respectability. We call it 'owning our personal power' or some other euphemism that sounds healthy and responsible and which reinforces the faulty premise that, given a choice, we'll do the right thing. C'mon. Who are we kidding?"

Most of the time when God forces me out of my comfortable cocoon to address ways I'm sabotaging my life with my "gotta be me" attitude, I hang on to the shell from the inside. He has to drag me kicking and screaming into that new place I need to go in order to be more like Him. I'm amazed He doesn't walk away in disgust.

There's a payoff for letting God call the shots instead of holding Him at arm's length.

- "... that you may be successful wherever you go." (Joshua 1:7)

- "... so that it may go well with you and your children." (Deuteronomy 4:40)

- ". . . whoever listens to me will live in safety."
  (Proverbs 1:33)

We don't get a pass on life's tough stuff, but, generally speaking, life flat out works better when we do it God's way. Since most of us were raised on rewards, the incentives may help.

In *The Ascent of a Leader*, the authors talk about the role of obedience in submitting to authority on the job. They say that biblical obedience has a bad reputation in many circles, but it doesn't mean what many people think it means.

> It does not mean setting aside our God-given right to question or appeal. It does not mean giving up our right to affect our own destiny. And it certainly was never intended to strip us of our sense of ownership in the work of our hands.
>
> Obedience from the heart does not mean a loss of self. Obedience from the heart does not mean compliance. Compliance sounds like, "OK, OK, I'll do it. But it won't be pretty." Obedience says, "I'll do this because I trust you, and believe it is for our best."[2]

So it is with obedience to God. It's saying that beyond any incentives or sense of "I have to do this because you're my boss," we obey because we trust Him and believe He knows what's best. He hasn't walked away despite all the ways we've pushed Him around. He's demonstrated He's deserving of our trust.

Feel like living dangerously? Tell God you're willing to conform your behavior to His expectations rather than expecting Him to conform His behavior to yours. Pursue wholehearted, *dangerous* devotion.

Reality

☐ Do you treat God like a consultant or like the CEO of your life?

☐ Have you obeyed all that He's already told you to do?

☐ Has your obedience been offered willingly, or is it a grudging compliance for fear of His wrath?

☐ What specific attitudes need to change?

☐ What's the hardest part of obeying Him?

☐ If this seems difficult, ask Him to reshape your view of obedience.

Finishing

The president of a high-tech start-up company once told me it took Alexander Graham Bell 200 tries to invent the telephone. When Graham was asked if he felt like a failure because it took so long, he reportedly replied, "Not at all! I learned 199 ways not to make a telephone."

The client loved the story because, like Alexander Graham Bell, he and his colleagues shared a similar determination. They too worked in the telecommunications field, except they are developing solutions to problems that plague wireless phones.

This same man has a collection of pigs in his office—a stuffed pig, a ceramic pig, a pig that asks for money. He uses the pig metaphor in memos and meetings to represent the kind of no-nonsense, roll-up-your-sleeves, never-give-up attitude he says it takes to be successful.

What drives people to persevere? Psychologists are quick to recite all the reasons people fail to stick with something to the end. A fear of failure. Not feeling worthy of the success that might follow meeting a goal. Lack of hope about the future. Fear of not having anything to live for once an objective is met.

Those are helpful markers for monitoring our own pattern of stops and starts, but I'm more interested in why people *don't* give up, especially those who persevere when no guaranteed reward awaits them—people like Mother Theresa, who labored forty years on the streets of Calcutta before the world took notice.

Take the apostle Paul. It's no surprise why he succeeded early in his adult life before he became a Christian, when he went by the name Saul. He was brilliant and driven, and he moved in the right circles and seemed well on the road to fulfilling his ambitions. Gamaliel, the most honored rabbi of the first century, was his mentor.

He taught in synagogues and amphitheaters and was widely respected as a true Jewish intellectual. His pals, the Pharisees, especially loved how doggedly Paul hunted down Christians to have them killed. The guy had success written all over him. Persevering under those conditions, however, was not a tough gig.

Then one day, when Saul was traveling to Damascus, God showed up in a blinding, flashing light so fierce it either knocked Saul down or he fell down in sheer terror. God wanted Saul's attention—and that would definitely get my attention.

God wanted Saul to know who was really in charge. In the process, He gave Saul a new name, Paul. Suddenly, the anti-Christian zealot was singing a different tune. He couldn't shut up about how God had changed his heart and could do the same for anyone—including the hated Gentiles. The Pharisees were not amused.

Paul's God-encounter marked him for life, which was probably a good thing since nothing in Paul's life would ever be the same. The events after his conversion read like a soap opera. He was repeatedly beaten, stoned and imprisoned. Then comes the incredible drama played out in Acts chapters 23-28. Forty Jews formed a conspiracy and vowed not to eat until Paul was dead. They'd had about enough of his newfound faith. It took more than 400 Roman soldiers to spirit Paul into the protective custody of Felix, governor of Judea.

Over the next couple years, Paul appeared before a parade of Roman officials as his old Pharisee pals falsely accused him of being a troublemaker and a ringleader who started riots. Technicalities and the Romans' desire to pacify the Jews kept Paul in jail unjustly until finally the officials threw up their hands and shipped him off for trial in Rome as Paul had requested. He knew he'd never get a fair trial in Jerusalem on the trumped-up charges.

Paul joined a ship with other prisoners bound for Rome. They were buffeted by constant storms that slowed their journey, but instead of docking in a safe harbor for the winter, they pressed on. A nasty hurricane bounced them all over the Adriatic Sea for fourteen days. Things got so bad that even fearless Paul thought the end was near.

God sent an angel to reassure Paul everyone would survive but that their troubles were far from over. A major shipwreck followed. What kept Paul going? Was it remembering what happened on the road to Damascus years earlier? Was he simply too afraid of God to give up? I believe it was actually the unrelenting hail of dire circumstances that cemented him to God.

Paul knew that his compelling oratory, brilliant intellect and considerable leadership skills were not enough to take him across the finish line—not under these conditions. He would make it because He was committed to something bigger than himself—to God's goals and not his own. God had promised to stick with Paul if Paul stuck with Him until the job was done. Paul hung on to God and never looked back.

When Saul the cosmopolitan Roman citizen and admired intellectual became Paul the Christian zealot, what happened to him was nothing any of us would choose. No one aspires to downward mobility. Still, Paul never backed off an inch. Furthermore, he also saw God do things, and he personally experienced things he could never have imagined in his wildest dreams. Life with God was quite a ride.

Incredibly, way back at the beginning of this drama, on the eve of his trip to Jerusalem where this Acts 23-28 saga began, Paul told church leaders,

> I am going to Jerusalem, not knowing what will happen to me there. I only know that in every city the Holy Spirit warns me that prison and

hardships are facing me. However, I consider my life worth nothing to me, if only I may finish the race and complete the task the Lord Jesus has given me. (20:22-24)

Get the job done for God, Paul says. That's the bottom line. The rest is window dressing. Cling to God as if your life depends on it—because it does.

We need heroes who set the bar high and spur us to excel. I admire the achievements of brilliant, inventive and determined people like Alexander Graham Bell and my friend, the high-tech entrepreneur. But frankly, when the shipwreck seasons of my life come along, I'm with Paul. I plan to stay close to God and hang on for dear life. I'm mastering a God-grip that would make Paul proud.

Reality

☐ Who is a Christian in your life you think will finish well?

☐ What specifically do you admire about them?

☐ Name your current character traits that might handicap you if you experienced a shipwreck season.

☐ Set aside time in the next week to use a concordance and investigate Scripture that addresses your issue. Write a paragraph to yourself about how you want to finish your life.

The View from My Heart

My dad was a salesman, an extraordinary salesman. He could make you glad you spent your last dollar buying a set of pots and pans you didn't need. At the age of sixty-nine, he underwent a heart transplant that was an act of salesmanship all by itself since heart transplants, at that time, were not typically performed on anyone over fifty-five. A world-renowned heart transplant surgeon agreed to operate on Dad because Dad believed the surgery would be successful. The doctor said his positive attitude would make a world of difference in his long-term prognosis. And it did.

A couple years after Dad's surgery, when I was working in public relations, one of my first clients was a company solely devoted to selling motivational materials that espoused the same kind of possibility thinking Dad embraced. Every month they mailed more than a million catalogs to people who spent, on average, a couple hundred dollars a year to learn more about the power of positive thinking.

Spurred on by Dad's example and intrigued by my client's robust success, I began to listen to dozens of these motivational tapes. Speaker after speaker told me there were no obstacles in life—only opportunities. What the mind could dream up and believe in, it could achieve. It was very convincing stuff. I was ready to start a revolution.

Just as I was about to hop aboard the Positive Thinkers Bandwagon, I was diagnosed with the melanoma mentioned in an earlier chapter. The virulent skin cancer required two major surgeries and six weeks on my back so the skin grafts on my leg could heal.

Within a few months of my bout with cancer, Dad died—good attitude and all. His death was followed a month later by the sudden and unexpected death of one of my best friends. She was forty-two. She left behind a devastated husband and two teenagers. A month after that, I contracted shingles. Try as I might, I saw no positive opportunity in any of it.

I know attitude matters. Wallowing in despair never helped anyone climb out of it. Charles Swindoll says that, when we can't change the inevitable, "the only thing we can do is play on the one string we have. And that is our attitude."

Nevertheless, slapping on a Happy Face doesn't cut it for me. Does being a child of God mean never having to say you're angry? Disappointed? Hurting?

I met Joni Eareckson Tada at a conference not long ago where we were both speakers. Joni has a remarkable international ministry in spite of severe physical disabilities that have confined her to a wheelchair for three decades. She requires help from others to do everything but sleep.

She always sounds so upbeat on her radio program. And, in person, she has a smile and personality that fills a room. I wondered how she felt when no one else was around.

Over lunch, with her trademark honesty, she described what it's like each morning. After her husband leaves for work, a friend arrives to bathe and dress her. The friend puts on Joni's makeup, brushes her hair and her teeth and helps launch her day.

"I often start the day feeling I have no resources—no smile, nothing," she says. "That's when I tell God I need His. Whatever joy you see is hard won every day." That's an attitude with its feet firmly planted in reality. It acknowledges the way things are and admits that happy talk is not enough to carry most of us through life's deep valleys.

I wish Habakkuk could have had lunch with Joni and me. He and Joni would have completely understood each other. The Old Testament prophet argued with God over the injustices he witnessed, moaning that life was definitely not fair. But in Habakkuk 3:17-19 he concluded,

> Though the fig tree does not bud
>   and there are no grapes on the vines,
> though the olive crop fails
>   and the fields produce no food,
> though there are no sheep in the pen
>   and no cattle in the stalls,
> yet I will rejoice in the LORD,
>   I will be joyful in God my Savior.

> The Sovereign LORD is my strength;
> he makes my feet like the feet of a deer.

"No matter how bad it gets, Lord, I won't lose heart," he said. His confidence was not in his ability to recast his circumstances into some grand adventure. His confidence was in the One who governs all circumstances. I can live with hope, Habbakuk said, because Someone smarter than me sees the big picture and has everything under control. It helped Habakkuk feel secure and sure-footed, like a deer.

Not long ago I saw a documentary about the light-houses of Maine. The narrator explained that light-houses are more complex than they look. For example, it's not the wattage of the light atop the lighthouse that determines how brightly it shines. It's the light-house lenses that focus and amplify the light. There are nine grades and dozens of exquisite patterns to the hand-cut lenses. They are the single most important factor affecting how far and how accurately the light-house "sees."

Like the lighthouse, the quality and tone of my life will not be determined by how brightly (or positively) I view life. Rather, it will come from the lens through which I see my life.

I want to see through the same lens Habakkuk and Joni use, confident that God knows what He's doing, and life is brighter with Him than any of the alternatives.

Reality

- [ ] Through what kind of lens do you look at life?

- [ ] Would your present attitude sustain you if you were a quadriplegic?

- [ ] Have you placed your confidence in confidence instead of in God? If so, what are its benefits, and what are its drawbacks?

- [ ] Where in your thinking do you need to make an adjustment?

Angels Looking for Work

I heard about a little boy who asked God to send his parents $500 so they could pay the rent and buy groceries. The boy's father had lost his job, and the child thought that his request might carry more weight if instead of praying he wrote a letter to God.

Local postal workers, deeply touched by the family's need, collected $300 and mailed the money to the family "from God." The child shot off a note of thanks to God, adding, "Next time, though, don't go through the post office. They took $200 right off the top."

It's true. God delights in hearing our requests. He told us in Philippians 4:6 to ask for what we need. "Do not be anxious about anything, but in everything, by prayer and petition, with thanksgiving, present your requests to God." Nevertheless, prayer is more than requisitioning solutions like we order office supplies.

When my daughter started praying for the first time as a young child, she asked, "If God already knows everything, then why do I have to tell Him what I need? Isn't that wasting His time? And, if He's the boss and knows what's best, then He's probably already made up His mind what to do. Why bother telling Him what I want to happen?"

Honestly, haven't you wondered the same thing? What's the point of prayer if not to enlist God's buy-in, get His help to get something? If there's nothing to transact, why am I sitting here flapping my jaws? I know that's not the correct answer, but isn't that the attitude our prayers sometimes reflect?

Prayer has so much more to offer. It reminds us where answers are found. It's a way we can show God we want Him in charge. It acknowledges that our solutions are not as good as His. The main point of prayer, however, is the relationship. Oswald Chambers said, "The meaning of prayer is that we get hold of God, not of the answers."[1] God longs to relate to us on a deep, personal, gut-honest level. Intimacy is what He's after.

When I show up to meet with God, and all I have in mind is my grocery list of needs and prayer requests, I can almost picture Him saying wistfully, "Say, would you like to stay a little while longer and let Me know how you're doing? How's everything else going in your life? Are you happy? What's not working? Let's talk about it. I can help."

It's a bit incomprehensible when you think about it. The Creator of the Universe wants to hang out with me? The One who created the Grand Canyon and orchids and babies and sunsets? *That* God? You mean He won't think it's stupid that I'm afraid of computers even though I can manage a client's six-figure communications budget? You mean He's amused when I thank Him for making chocolate one of the four basic food groups? (It is, isn't it?)

Prayer, ultimately, is conversation with God—an interactive dialogue where the language and format isn't nearly as important as the personal one-on-one connection. Like any relationship, if it's healthy it will have ups and downs. It will have light-hearted moments and dark times. If it's a true relationship, there will be times of confrontation when the tables are turned and He has questions for me. The questions slow me down and reveal me to myself. Isn't that what best friends do?

If we haven't spent enough time to establish that kind of intimacy, approaching God can feel akin to spending time with distant relatives we see only on holidays. Their strong opinions and deeply held beliefs are a little scary. They're different. They don't feel like safe people to spend time with, much less enjoy.

Then, one day, we find ourselves caught in a corner with them for an extended conversation and learn, much to our surprise, that they aren't as scary as we thought. Our perceptions were wrong. It can be like that with God.

Years ago I interviewed the late legendary jazz singer Ella Fitzgerald for a news feature. As an onstage performer, her considerable musical gifts gave her complete command of the audience. She totally captivated those who flocked to hear her.

Offstage I expected to meet the same strong, confident woman. Instead, I found a gracious but extraordinarily shy person without much to say beyond what her music said for her. It took one-on-one time with her to form a more balanced and accurate picture. It's possible that failure to spend enough time with God in prayer is a perception problem as much as a time management or even an obedience problem.

We think of Him in His most obvious roles. He is God, our Provider—"And my God will meet all your needs according to his glorious riches in Christ Jesus" (Philippians 4:19). He is God, our Protector. Psalm 91:11 says, "For he will command his angels concerning you to guard you in all your ways." The different names of God mentioned in Scripture fill volumes. But God, my best friend and closest confidante? God-who-meets-me-where-I'm-at? Whoa, that's a little personal.

Think about the people you love and care most about in the whole world. How did you fall in love with them? You spent time with them—lots of open-ended time, sharing, listening and just being together. There were probably awkward moments at first or even difficult seasons in the relationship. But one day you rounded a corner, and the relationship fed something deep in your spirit that couldn't be fed any other way. This person was as essential to your life as oxygen. It felt like coming home.

Pursue God like that. He'll love you back. He has plenty of angels on standby to address the items on your prayer list. But it is *you* He's been waiting for. *You're* the top request on *His* wish list.

Reality

☐ Why do you pray?

☐ Does God get your premium time or the left-overs?

☐ Is it intimidating to think that God wants to spend time alone with you?

☐ Have you spent enough time with Him to know if your perception of Him is correct?

☐ What steps can you take to invigorate your prayer times with God?

Finding the Still Point

One of my closest friends is an executive coach who helps female CEOs get their lives under control. She works with them to identify personal core values, set goals for the future and eliminate impediments to their personal success.

One of the clarifying exercises she uses to help them is called "Clean Sweep." The clients survey 100 things in their lives to find out what's "in the way" of fulfillment of their dreams. The questions are loosely categorized around relationships, money, physical environment and overall well-being. Completing the exercise requires a temporary mental, emotional and physical halt to their lives. They must stop, get off by themselves and think. She says that for some of them it's the hardest thing they've ever done.

TIME editorial pundit Steve Lopez wrote recently, "Nobody, with the possible exception of Congress, knows how to do nothing anymore. . . . Whatever happened to the moment of quiet reflection and the slothful joy of idle thought?"[1]

The French have a phrase for it: *reculer pour mieux sauter*. "Draw back to jump higher." The Celts called it "thin time." No striving, pushing, persisting, thinking, talking or planning. Just delicious white space. Human beings are the only creatures to whom God gave the capacity to reflect. Unfortunately, our culture doesn't hold pausing in high regard. We honor productivity and action.

I met a man recently who leads a team of project engineers for a major corporation. He offered to give his people one paid day a month to reflect, if they promised not to use it to clean out the garage or take the kids to an amusement park. They actually had to go off alone somewhere, anywhere of their choosing, and think about their lives.

He didn't intend it as a spiritual exercise, although he encouraged them to think about more than just the job. Rather, it was designed to stop the racket and give his men and women a chance to focus on whatever it was in their lives that needed attention. He was convinced the fruit of that time apart would ultimately show up in their job performance in increased focus, productivity and improved interpersonal relationships.

In all the time he has extended the offer, he said, not a single engineer has taken him up on the offer. When he pressed to learn why, some said they had no idea what they'd do with eight hours of blank time when they weren't doing something—it sounded awful. Others said they couldn't afford the "down time." They perceived it as basically throwaway time—a luxury they couldn't afford.

I suppose we shouldn't be surprised. Our lives are held hostage by lists, appointments, goals and business plans where we can measure and quantify outcomes. How can you do a cost-benefit analysis of blank time and have it hold its own?

We bring the same mind-set to our drawing near to God—turning our quiet time into an elaborate program of worship music, Bible study, Scripture memorization and an intercessory prayer list that circles the globe. It's as if we believe there's an unspoken law that forbids a person to be alone with God unless he or she is doing something.

Dallas Willard says, "Solitude and silence train us to let go of thinking we have so much we have to do. That's a dangerous phrase. There is very little I have to do, and those things generally apply to my personal relationships."

Do we think God will be bored if nothing is happening? *He's got a lot on His plate. Wouldn't He rather be tending to some conflict in a war-torn third-world country or focusing on the millions of children who go to bed hungry every night? It doesn't seem right to take up His time unless I'm making it worth His while—you know, worshiping Him or soliciting His help or studying up on Him so my interactions will be more fruitful. After all, I would never dream of walking into the boss's office without an agenda.*

Another reason for our discomfort with solitude is a fear that maybe, if we're listening and not talking, we won't like what God has to say. If we see Him as the great Cosmic Thumb who can't wait to nail us about our inadequacies, who would want to put themselves in a room alone with Him? *If He doesn't nail me, He might ask me to do something I'd rather not do. I think it's better if I keep a little chit-chat going.*

Then there's always the nagging fear that He may say nothing at all. How will *that* feel? Besides, if we haven't made a practice of listening instead of doing all the talking, how would we recognize His voice?

In no time at all, we've built an ironclad case against solitude. Our loss.

Psalm 46:10 says, "Be still, and know that I am God." It implies there is something that happens in stillness and solitude, some understanding or sense of God, that cannot happen any other way.

In complete stillness, an intoxicating calm seeps in and soothes my jangled nerves. It's safe to exhale. I relocate the heart that's been hiding behind a bulletproof vest and traveling at Mach I for too long. There's room for a fresh start.

When I'm silent, I find God has a lot to say.

Reality

- [ ] How do you view solitude? Do you see its benefits as important enough to make it a priority?

- [ ] Are there things about solitude that make you anxious?

- [ ] Does "being" instead of "doing" feel like a waste of time?

- [ ] If this is a new practice, begin with a modest goal of ten to fifteen minutes a day. Use a psalm or worship music to move you toward silence. Tell God you're listening, and invite Him to speak to you however He chooses.

The Pain That Has No Name

The old cliché about the certainty of death and taxes leaves out the other inevitability of life—suffering. Thanks to cable television, the internet and other forms of global communication, we can now watch human tragedy as it's happening, twenty-four hours a day.

We know the Parade of Horribles has dulled our senses when our outrage is measured by the size of the body count—as if suffering needs a number to be legitimized.

A Pacific tsunami with waves the height of a five-story building hits the shores of Papua, New Guinea, and fifteen minutes later 2,200 people lay dead. Empty beaches remain where villages once stood. A missionary friend e-mails me to say entire families he knew have vanished.

In Afghanistan, windows of the homes where women live must be painted over so outsiders will never see them. Women must wear "silent shoes" so they'll never be heard. An angry mob beats a woman to death for accidentally exposing her arm while driving. To no one's surprise, suicide among women in Afghanistan is rampant.

In the office of a Christian medical relief organization, a young man from Sierra Leone, West Africa describes the reign of terror he's left behind, where civil war rages. In a voice barely above a whisper, he tells of the rape of women, the mutilation of babies and the starvation. He escaped with the help of international medical volunteers, but he's not sure about the safety of the extended family he left behind.

A friend of mine, juggling compassion fatigue on the one hand and his own suffering on the other, told me in a rare moment of self-revelation, "I know my problems are small by comparison, but they're not small to me. The truth is, sometimes all I can handle are my own problems."

While suffering comes in different portions, the pain that may be hardest to shake is the kind that's happening to us.

"I can't imagine what it would be like to be buried alive in an earthquake," my friend continued. "But I do know what it feels like to have my manager rag on me because I turned in expense reports that represent my actual expenses. I never thought I'd be in trouble for my honesty," he said, shaking his head. "The guy was angry because *my* expense reports called into question *his* expense reports. He's making my life miserable in a dozen different ways, not the least of which undermines my authority and leaves me out of all decision-making. It's humiliating, and I'm quickly becoming the outsider. Unfortunately, I'm not in a position where I can leave the job right now."

His wife is suffering too. She's in a profession where she bills her time. The senior partners are on her case, he says, for being too "literal" in her billing. They'd prefer she be a little more "creative." Her pain is in knowing she works hard and delivers superior work but may never become a partner in the firm because she doesn't play the game by their rules.

There are no organized prayer chains for this kind of suffering. You can't go to a card shop and select a greeting card that says, "My heart goes out to you for what it's costing you to live out your faith in the marketplace." It's a silent suffering that wears down our spirits like a low-grade fever.

"I don't feel right to call it suffering," he said. "There's too much real suffering in the world for this to qualify. But it hurts anyway—even if I have no bloody wound to show for it. And it doesn't go away."

God doesn't explain His actions or inaction, attentiveness or inattentiveness. In those moments of injustice and suffering when we're left without answers, it helps to look at our circumstances in the light of God's larger, overarching plan, a plan that stretches far into eternity.

In Second Corinthians 4:17-18, Paul says suffering may be unfair, but it's never pointless. It's preparation. "These little troubles are getting us ready for an eternal glory that will make all our troubles seem like nothing. Things that are seen don't last forever, but things that are not seen are eternal. That's why we keep our minds on the things that cannot be seen." (CEV)

Your current problems are only a small piece of the puzzle, Paul says. Get the Big Picture. Take the long view.

How ironic. Taking the long view is a business strategy long held by America's most successful companies. In the business classic *Built to Last*, the authors studied characteristics of companies that stayed on top over the long haul. "Contrary to popular wisdom," the authors say, "the proper first response to a changing world is not to ask, 'How should we change?' but rather to ask, 'What do we stand for and why do we exist?' This should never change."[1]

In other words, the authors found that visionary companies had timeless core values and an enduring purpose. It helped them weather fluctuating market conditions, competition, management changes, financial difficulty and a host of other problems.

Your core values and enduring purpose as a person who has a relationship with Christ will help you weather difficulties and endure for the long haul too. Plus, you have the presence of the Holy Spirit in your heart as God's reminder that you will not suffer a single minute alone. Not only that, the Bible says Christ sits at God's right hand and constantly intercedes on our behalf.

In other words, the invisible pain may be around awhile, but you have a companion for the journey, and there's an Advocate who's gone on ahead to plead your case to the One in Charge.

Your long-term outlook is good, and the hard part won't last forever. He promised.

Reality

☐ Is there invisible suffering in your life?

☐ Which of your personal core values puts you at odds with the world around you?

☐ Have you taken the long view?

☐ Have you made judgments about God's concern for you based on action He has or has not taken?

☐ What is the truth about God?

☐ Tell Him where you're hurting right now. Sit quietly in His presence for a few minutes, and ask Him to comfort you.

The View from the Bench

D on't expect to learn patience on the job. Think about it. Have you ever heard a CEO tell stockholders, "We adopted a strategy of waiting this year, and our stock doubled in value." On the contrary, companies advertise *fast* shipping, *fast* food, *fast* service. The hottest new business magazine is *Fast Company*. "Patience," one client told me, "is for soufflé chefs. I don't wait for a three-minute egg."

I've spent my entire adult life in time-sensitive or deadline-oriented jobs. During my years in radio, the goal was not only to get the story, but to get it on the air as fast as possible—especially faster than the competition.

It amused me when I covered a breaking story and interviewed someone unfamiliar with the nature of the news business. "Can I get back to you tomorrow?" they'd say. *Tomorrow?* I'd think. *This story will have a beard on it by lunchtime.* That's why journalists are pushy.

When I left broadcasting and returned to a traditional business career, the action didn't stop. One of my areas of specialty was crisis management—helping companies manage a product tampering or a plant explosion or a strike or an accident in the operating room. Quick and decisive action was critical. You dared not wait to act unless you wanted to be buried. The whole point was to get out in front of the story.

That's why waiting is not my favorite thing to do. It's a big jolt to show up on God's doorstep ready to do business and learn that God is not "on deadline." He's not in a hurry. He feels no pressure to act because of circumstances. In fact, waiting is one of His most effective ways to remind me I'm not in charge.

Waiting gets our attention. It forces us to stand with empty hands until God decides to fill them. It gives God room to turn the spotlight from our circumstances to the state of our heart. What happens in us while we wait is often more important than what we're waiting for. It's definitely not downtime.

God made Elijah wait when Elijah desperately wanted God to act. It started in First Kings 18 when the prophet stood up to 850 false prophets who worshiped Baal. To expose Baal as a fake, Elijah staged one of the most dramatic showdowns in the Bible. Both sides built wooden altars and placed a sacrificial calf on each one. Both asked their God to ignite their altar. Whichever altar caught fire would prove who was the one true God.

The false prophets spent hours shouting prayers and working themselves into a lather trying to cajole their god, Baal, to deliver the goods. Elijah loved every minute of their misery, taunting them mercilessly. "What's the problem, guys? Is your God asleep? Maybe you need to shout a little louder."

When it was Elijah's turn, he raised the stakes by soaking his altar with water before inviting God to demonstrate His power. Elijah's altar burst into flames. The crowd went bananas—and turned their hearts back to God. It would have been a great story for Elijah to tell his grandchildren, if only it had ended there.

The 850 false prophets were killed a short time later. An enraged Jezebel, worshiper of Baal, put out a contract on Elijah for eliminating her entire workforce. After an all-too-brief moment of victory, Elijah was running for his life.

Elijah's job was Spokesperson for God. He had risen to the challenge and demonstrated extraordinary courage and obedience in facing down the false prophets. Now he needed God to save him from Jezebel, and God seemed in no hurry to act.

Have you ever felt like you were standing up for God on the job—against all odds—while the bad guys were eating you for lunch? Have you prayed, asking God to solve a problem, and felt like He's hit the snooze button? Now you know how Elijah felt.

Although God didn't send in a SWAT team to rescue Elijah, He was not absent. Elijah was physically and emotionally depleted from his big showdown. First Kings 19:5-7 says God gave Elijah time to sleep. Then God sent an angel to feed Elijah. It didn't change Elijah's circumstances, but it did give him strength to go on.

Elijah had to travel forty more days before God provided a long-term solution to his life-threatening circumstances. Even then, when God finally spoke, it was not in the wind or the earthquake or the fire, but in a quiet whisper.

God wasn't throwing His weight around or being capricious. He tenderly ministered to Elijah's physical exhaustion and emotional distress. He gave Elijah a hideout and alerted Elijah when He was about to pay a visit (" . . . for the LORD is about to pass by," 19:11). But God addressed Elijah's problem His way on His timetable. There was no question who was in charge.

I suspect that if Elijah had his druthers, he still would have preferred God act a little more promptly. But Elijah saw a whole different side of God as he waited. He learned God isn't just around for life's mainstage events. He's also God on those days we're running for our lives.

Reality

- ☐ In what areas of your life do you feel God is dragging His feet?

- ☐ How have you viewed the waiting?

- ☐ What do you think God wants to teach you through this season of waiting that couldn't be learned any other way?

- ☐ Is it possible God keeps putting you in a holding pattern because He can't get your attention any other way? Ask Him.

I run in the path of your commands,
for you have set my heart free.
Psalm 119:32

Endnotes

PART ONE:
Taming Our Inner World

Ambition

1. Eugene H. Peterson, *A Long Obedience in the Same Direction* (Downers Grove, IL: InterVarsity Press, 1980), p. 149.

Arrogance

1. Oswald Chambers, *My Utmost for His Highest* (Uhrichsville, OH; Barbour and Company, Inc. 1963), p. 243.

Failure

1. F. Richard Ciccone, "Q & Q with James Edgar," *Chicago Tribune*, January 3, 1999, n.p.

Fear

1. Bill Hewitt, Alec Marr, Dina Shiloah, Lyndon Stambler and Eric Francis, *People*, December 20, 1999, pp. 153-156.

Insecurity

1. Team Reporters, "Gentle Genius," *People*, February 8, 2000, pp. 52-59.

Perfectionism

1. Philip Yancey, *What's So Amazing About Grace?* (Grand Rapids, MI: Zondervan Publishing House, 1997), p. 61.

Regret

1. Editors, "25 Ways to Re-Invent Yourself," *Modern Maturity*, January-February, 2000, pp. 38-41.
2. Gerald L. Sittser, *A Grace Disguised* (Grand Rapids, MI: Zondervan Publishing House, 1995), pp. 84, 85, 99.

PART TWO:
Taming Our Outer World

Balance

1. Nina Munk, "Finished at Forty: Suspect Age Bias?" *Fortune*, February 1, 1999, pp. 50-66.
2. C.S. Lewis, *Mere Christianity* (New York: Macmillan Publishing Co., 1960), p. 36.

Flexibility

1. Henry T. Blackaby and Claude V. King, *Experiencing God: Knowing and Doing the Will of God* (Nashville, TN: LifeWay Press, 1990), pp. 127-128.

Prejudice

1. Philip Yancey, "Getting to Know Me," *Christianity Today*, October 25, 1999, online archives.

Stress

1. M. Craig Barnes, *Yearning* (Downers Grove, IL: InterVarsity Press, 1991), p. 41.
2. Dr. Thomas H. Homes, "What Types of Stress Will Make You Sick?" *Good Health* magazine, August 8, 1989, n.p.

Success

1. Verla Gillmor, "Need a Confidence Boost?" *Today's Christian Woman*, May/June, 2000, pp. 44-47.
2. Tom Paterson, *Living the Life You Were Meant to Live* (Nashville, TN: Thomas Nelson, Inc. 1998), p. 38.

PART THREE:
Spiritual Flashpoints

Accountability

1. John Ortberg, Laurie Pederson, Judson Poling, *Pursuing Spiritual Transformation: Living in Jesus' Name* (South Barrington, IL: Willow Creek Community Church, 1997), p. 42.

Character

1. Verla Gillmore, "Chicago Hope," *Christianity Today*, September 6, 1999, pp. 74-82.

Community

1. Wray Herbert, "When Strangers Become Family," *U.S. News & World Report*, November 29, 1999, pp. 58-67.
2. Larry Crabb, *The Safest Place on Earth* (Nashville, TN: Word Publishing, 1999), p. 32.

Contentment

1. Amy Saltzman, *Downshifting: Reinventing Success on a Slower Track* (New York: Harper Collins Publishers, 1991), p. 14.

Gratitude

1. Buzz Aldrin as told to John Sherrill, "Communion in Space," *Guideposts* (New York: Guideposts Publishing, 1970), p. 3.

Obedience

1. C.S. Lewis, *The Lion, the Witch and the Wardrobe* (New York: Macmillan Publishing Co, Inc., 1999), p. 104.
2. Bill Thrall, Bruce McNicol and Ken McElrath, *The Ascent of a Leader* (San Francisco, CA: Jossey-Bass Publishers, Inc., 1999), p. 104.

Prayer

1. Oswald Chambers, *My Utmost for His Highest* (Uhrichsville, OH: Barbour and Company, Inc., 1963), p. 27.

Solitude

1. Steve Lopez, "Nothing Means Something," *TIME*, April 5, 1999, p. 20.

Suffering

1. James C. Collins and Jerry I. Porras, *Built to Last* (New York: HarperBusiness, 1997), p. xiv.